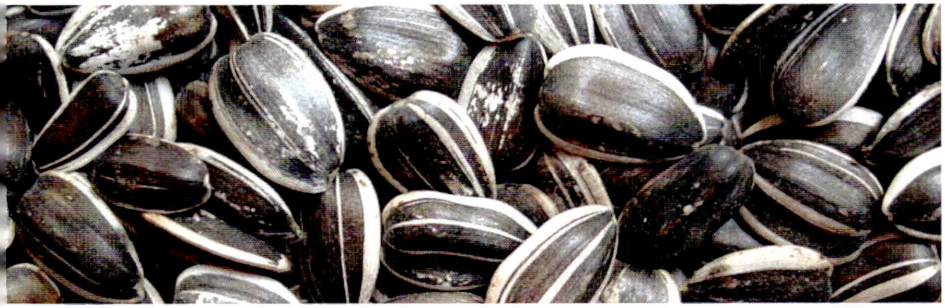

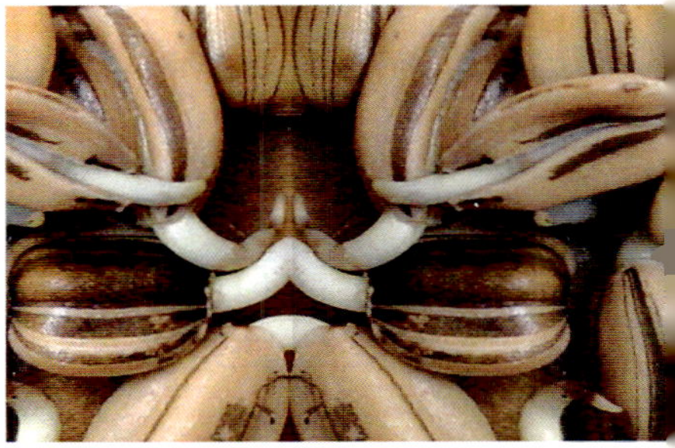

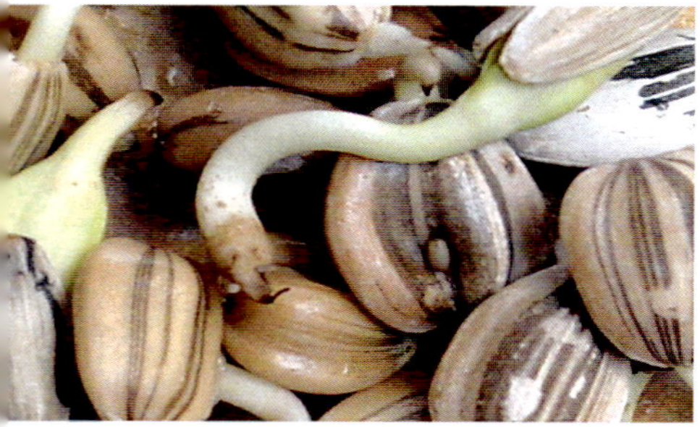

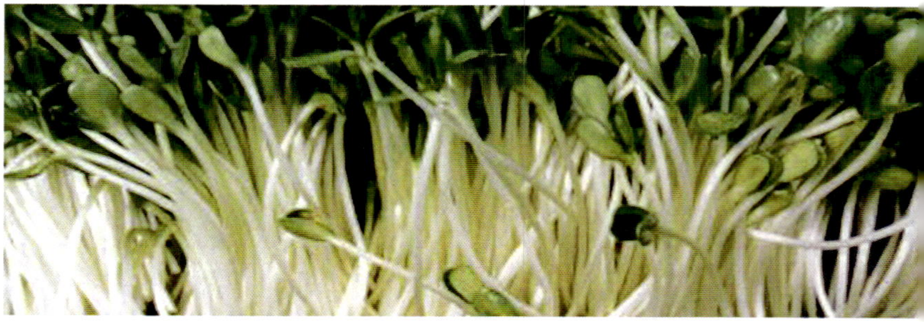

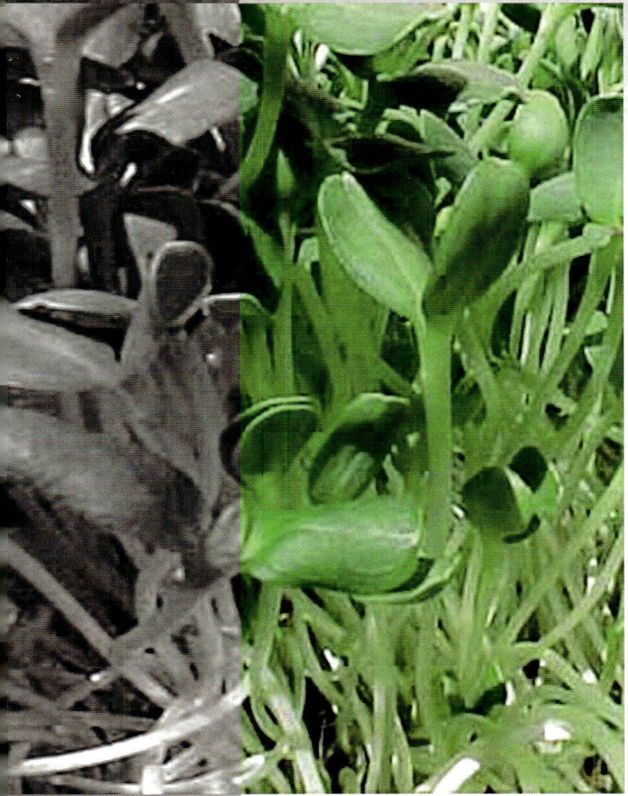

Messages from the Flower Pulpit

Joan Lederman

FIRST PAPERBACK EDITION
Printed in the United States of America

ISBN 978-0-6151-4116-9

The Soft Earth Press is a division of The Soft Earth
P.O. Box 252
Woods Hole MA 02543
508 540-5237
www.thesoftearth.com

Contents

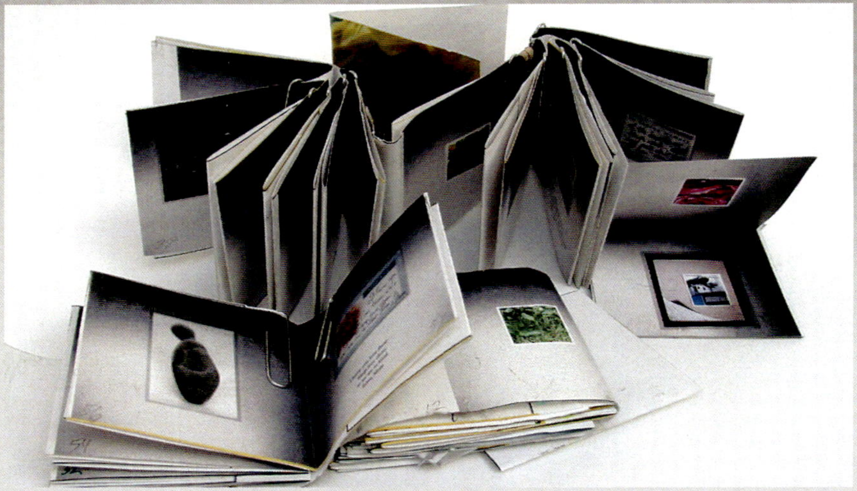

Dedication

for stories happening now,
for how we humans listen and glow,
and for our hospitable Earth

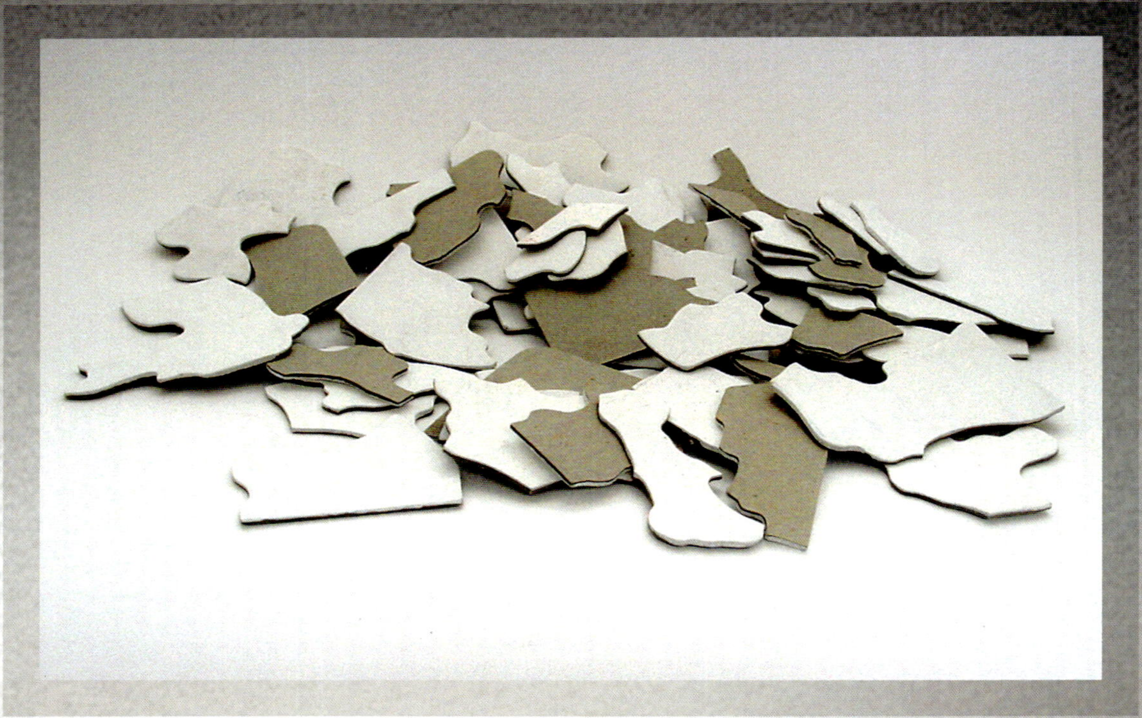

Introduction

The Process:

This book grew from a collection of 20 cards I wrote to myself when I gave myself flowers, mostly during the last five months of my mother Esther's life. Some I wrote on rare occasions in the following years. I have collected photos for thirty years. When the book emerged during the darkest days of winter, images clustered in my mind, especially at dawn between being awake and asleep.

Inspiration:

At the market, Astrid's flower concession comes after the entrance, a visual banquet where I get a whiff of some essence that helps me process everyday experience. I always visit with the flowers. Their luminosity attracts me in mysterious ways, and sometimes I buy flowers.

My favorite is the most mixed colors of roses, which Astrid sometimes assembled for me. Card writing began while she wrapped them, as she stood on a platform a step up from the floor. She and I chitchatted while I picked a card and wrote. Sometimes I was there alone. The cards reappeared on my desk during monthly purse dumpings, when I put them in a bright orange envelope. They were lost in my office behind my passport for a few years.

History:

Twenty years earlier I lived alone for five years in a rustic studio by the ocean. On this Juniper Point peninsula, I met my musician husband Perry on Christmas day. We became friends that winter, lovers during the full force of spring, moved to a house in autumn, and joyfully birthed our daughter Rayna the next spring. Fast forward a few years and Perry was diagnosed with cancer. Treatments and remissions continued for seven years until he died when Rayna was twelve. I had no idea how I alone could support a life three people had built together. Rayna and I couldn't live at my rented studio, and without new construction and expense, I couldn't work at home.

I was overwhelmed and anxious and a few people suggested I get medication. I researched a few recommended pharmaceuticals on the Internet. As I read, my anxiety increased and I slipped through cyberspace to a Web site with a bulleted list of natural alternatives.

There and then, I got the message that I could easily help myself. Recommendations included taking warm baths, exercising, playing, socializing, and buying myself flowers. Although I wanted to do these things, I first needed to address how I talked to myself. At this time I was listening to an inner voice who was demanding, unrealistic, judgmental, and who wasn't scheduling my time in ways that were kind.

Help came in various ways, and included a series of ten phone coaching sessions, a gift from friend Ted, after Perry died. Coach Carol, whom I never met, asked me to write a five-year plan and a one-year plan. I resisted but I did it. I sketched out a year, month by month. At July I wrote, "Smell the roses." Whoops! Aside from wild rugosa, I had no roses to smell. I was setting myself up to fail by planning to harvest roses I hadn't planted.

THEN, I understood the point of strategic planning. I went back to May, and wrote, "Buy rose bushes." On Mother's Day, I planted a group of three, which I chose for their aromas, and gave to myself as a gift.

Messages from the Pulpit

Card writing began nine years later, when my mother was old and slipping away from health. I knew we had little time together. She gave me some special things, which I drove home to Massachusetts from Florida in the car she gave me. Cargo included an asymmetrical handblown cobalt blue glass vase that I had always loved. I wrapped it in some of her still-fragrant clothes.

When I returned home, I couldn't let the vase be empty -- NOT YET.

That's when flower card writing began, like a lifeline to her as she faded. I realized the ordinary nature of generations coming and going, especially the nature of being a daughter and a mother. I learned how the body dies while the person heals. I learned my need to speak to myself as my mother had, as I saw it emerge on the gift cards. It became the "pulpit," because there something special happened. It was a simple ritual, like an opening in time, where I felt connected to all family, all space, and all time.

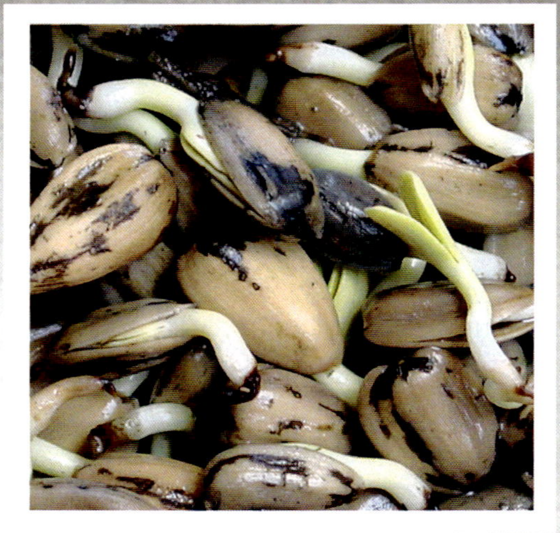

Choice

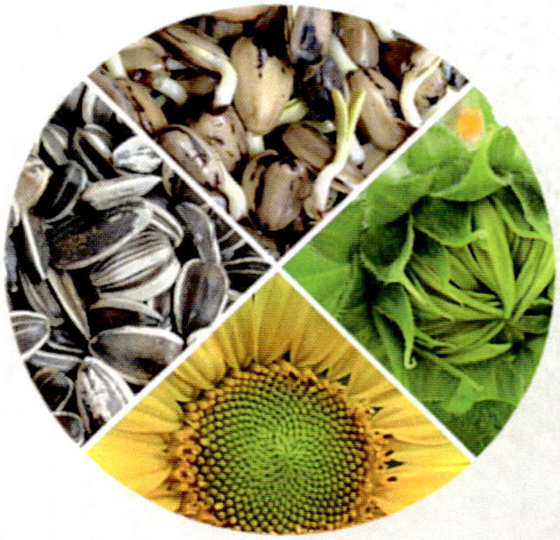

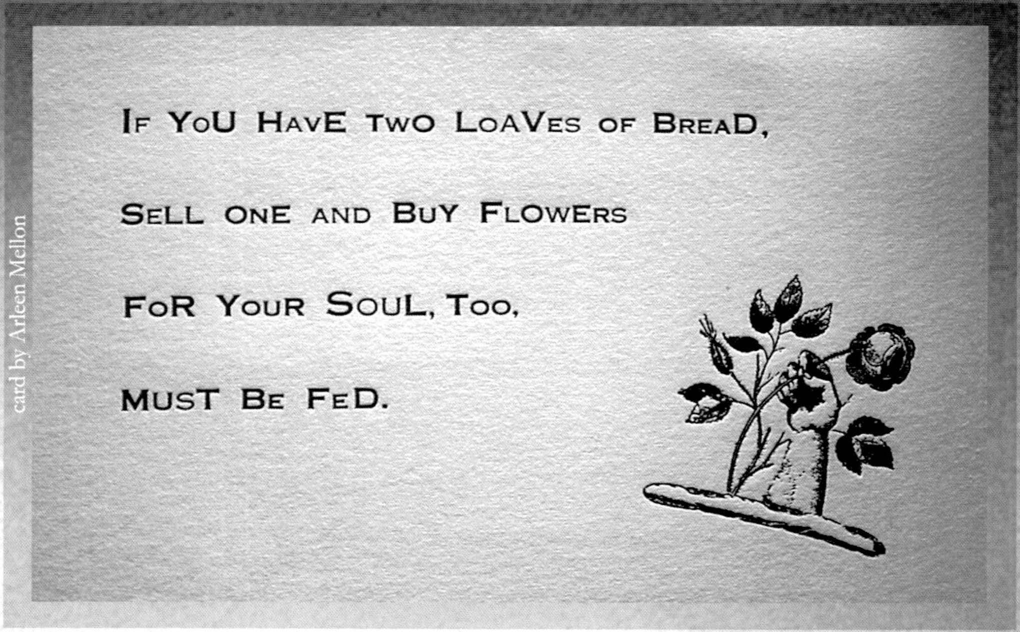

card by Arleen Mellon

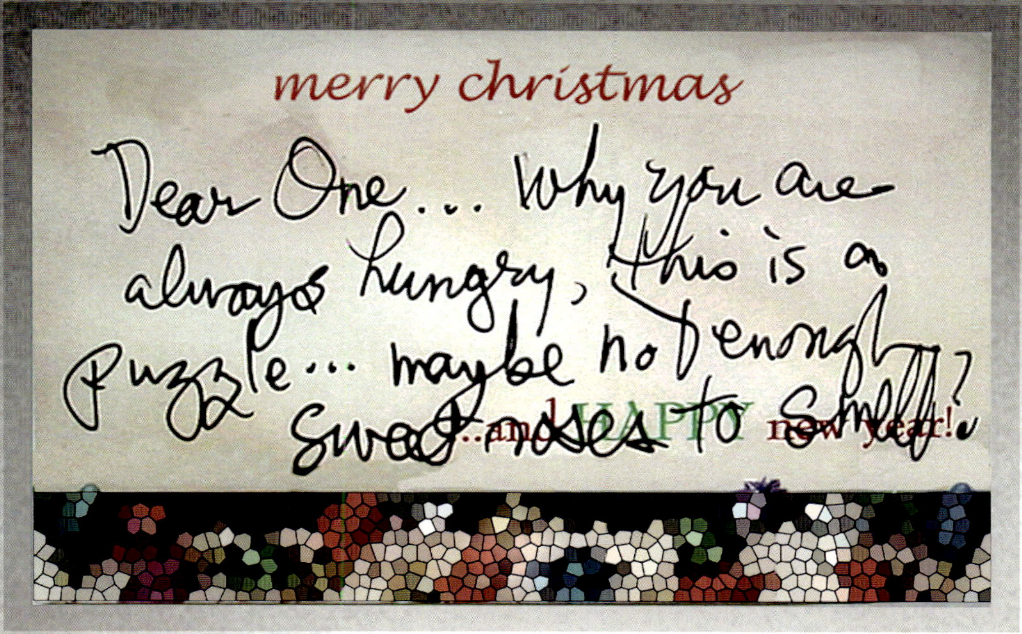

Dear One . . . why are you always hungry,
this is a puzzle . . . maybe
not enough sweet roses to smell?

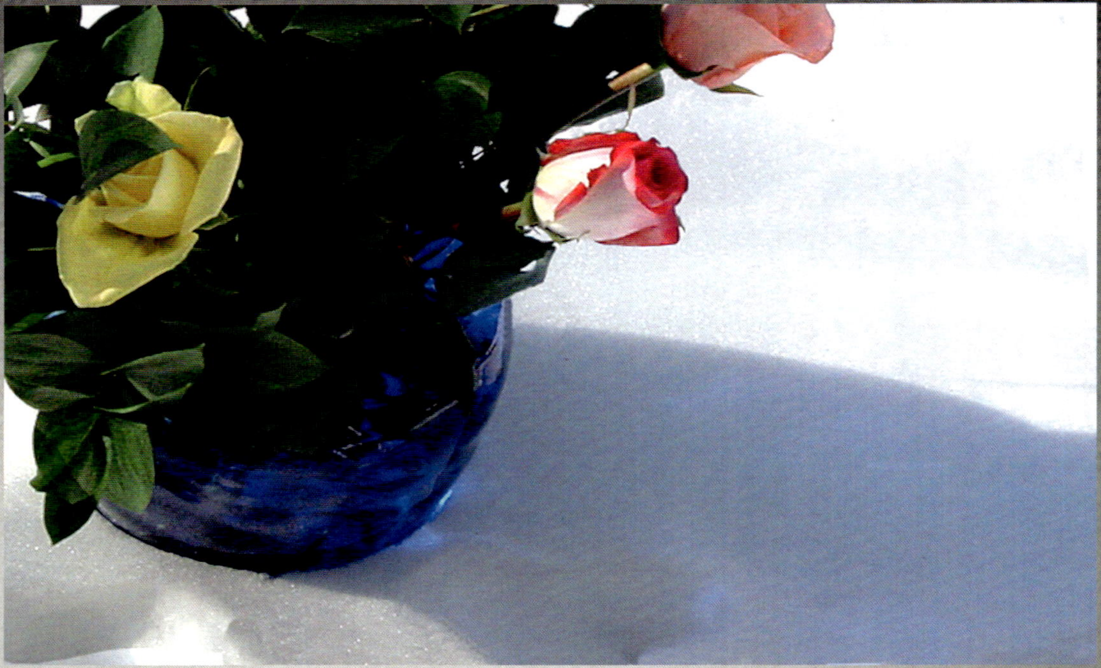

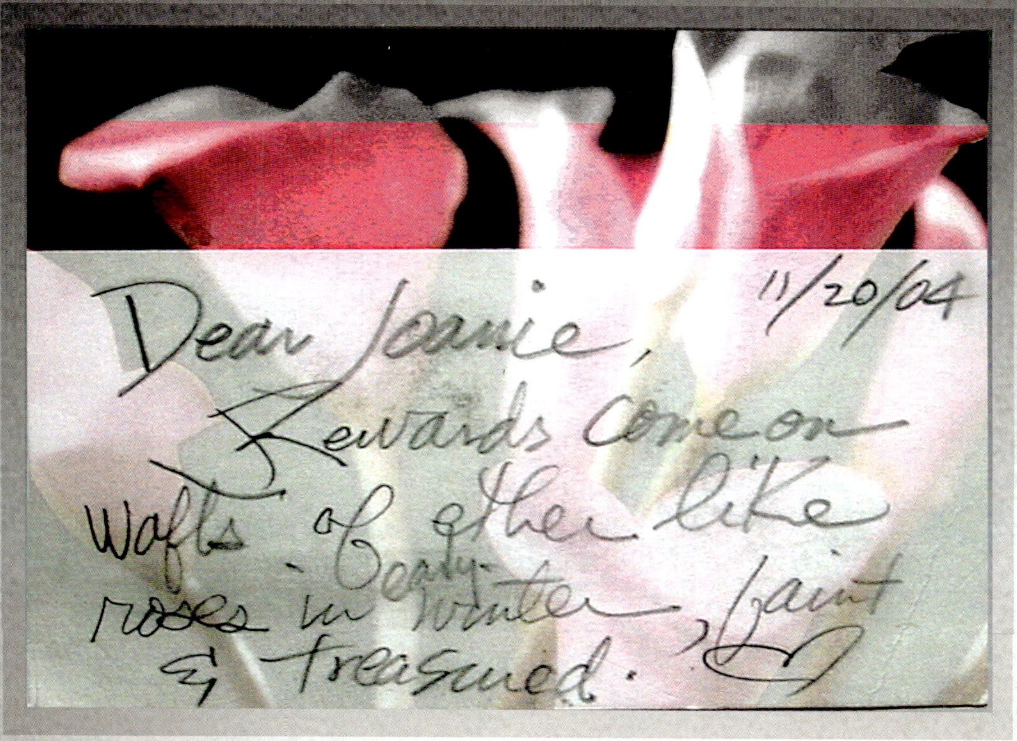

Dear Joanie,
Rewards come on wafts of ether
like roses in early winter,
faint & treasured.

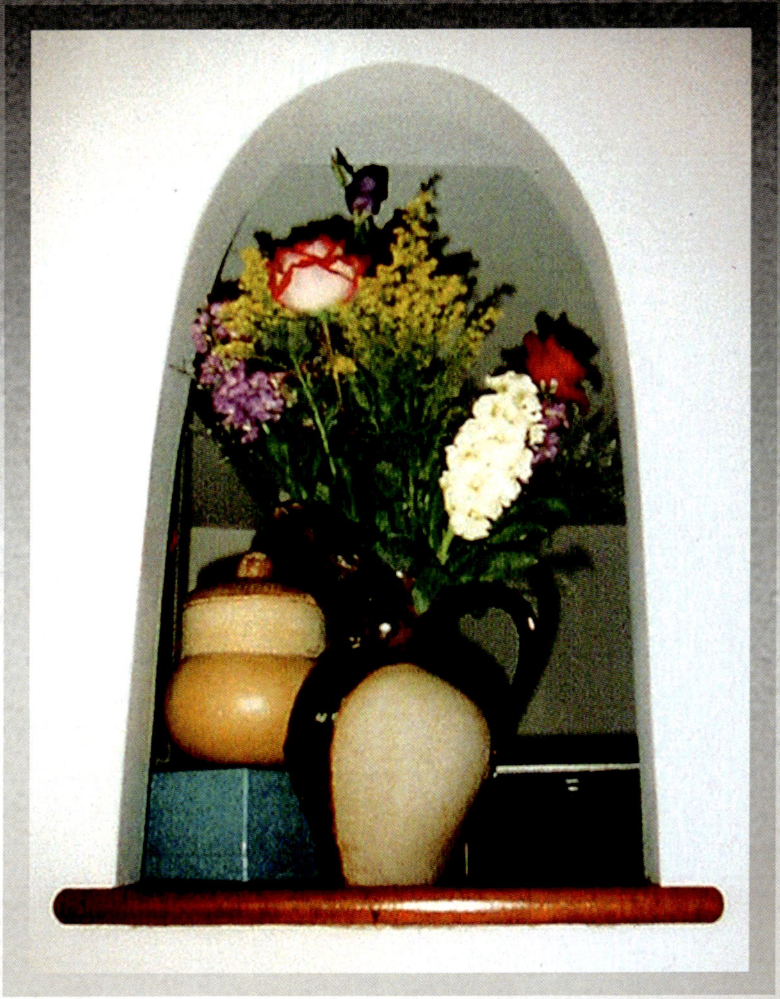

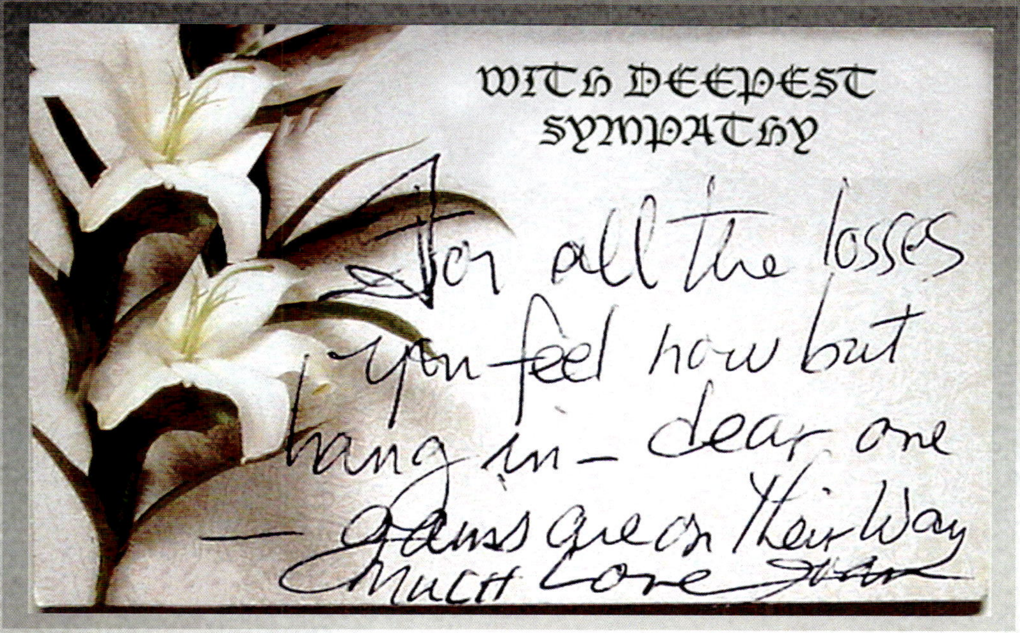

With deepest sympathy for all the losses
you feel now but hang in ~ dear one ~
gains are on their way.
MUCH Love, Joan

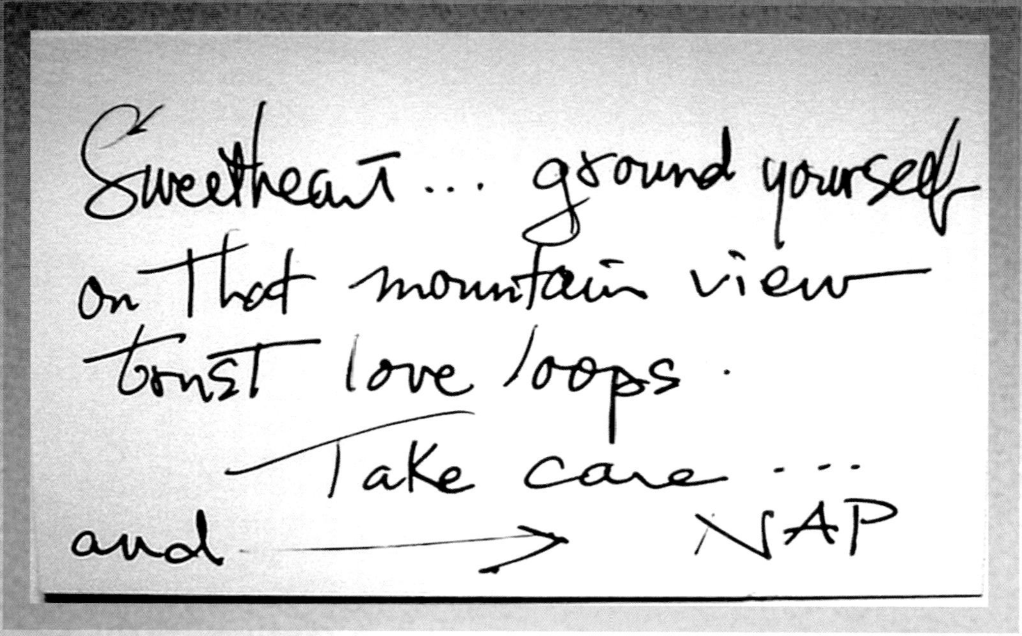

Sweetheart . . . ground yourself
on that mountain view, trust love loops.
Take care . . .
and ⟶ NAP

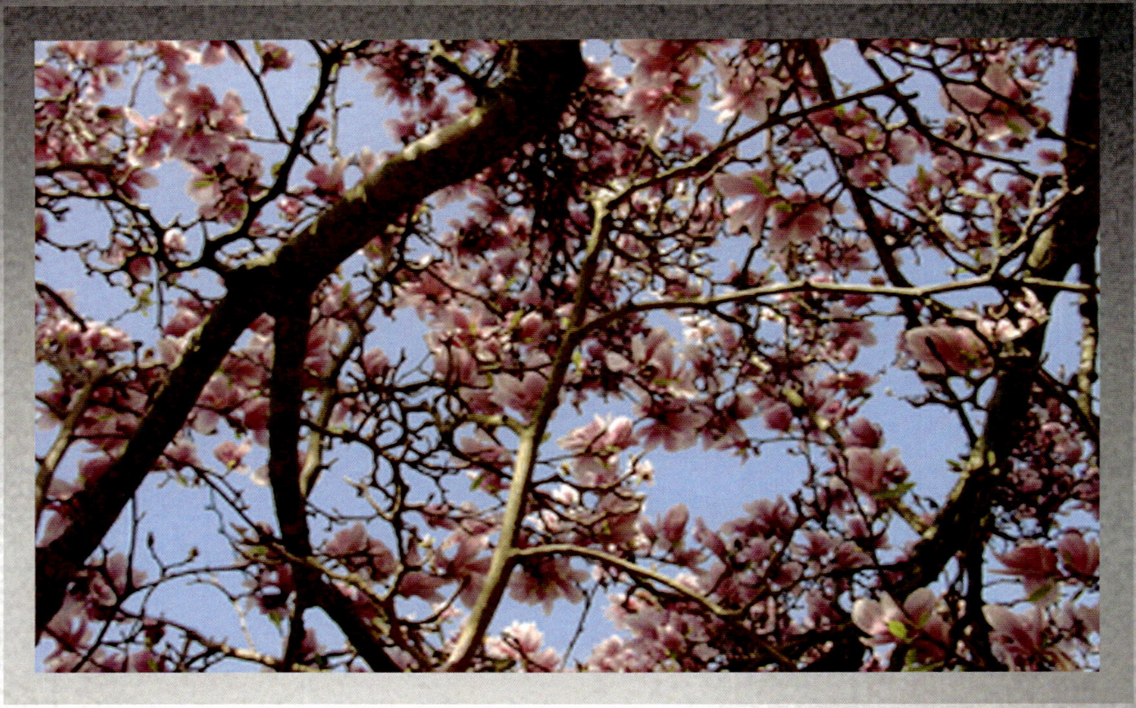

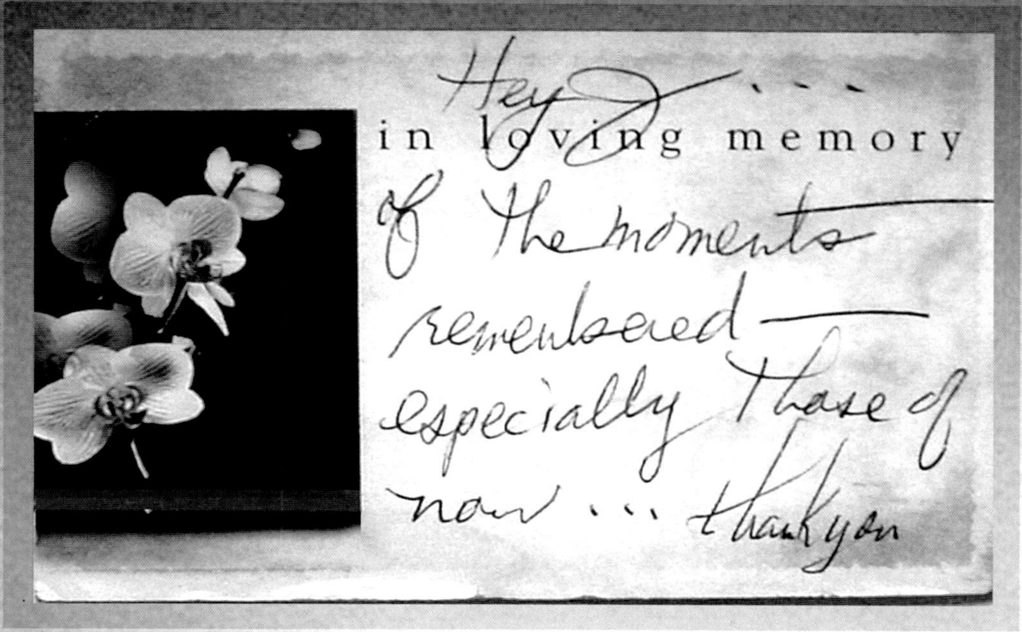

Hey J . . .
in loving memory of the moments
remembered – especially those of
now . . . thank you.

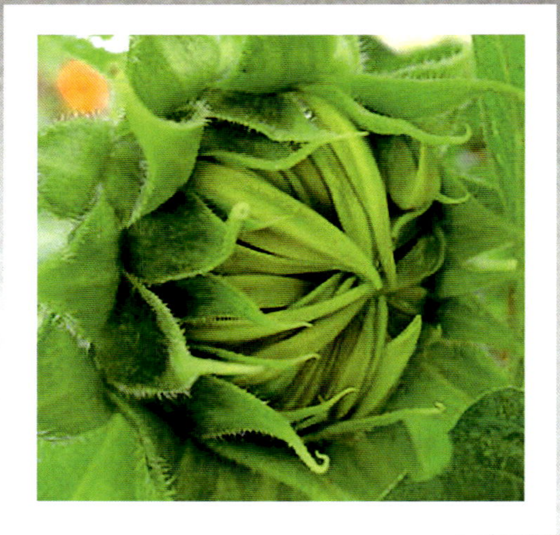

Friends

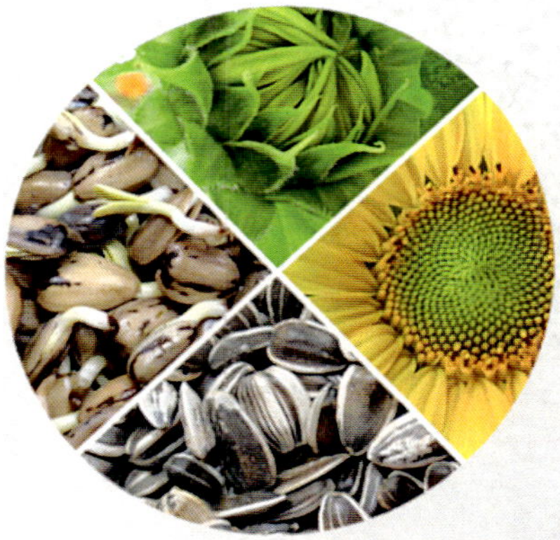

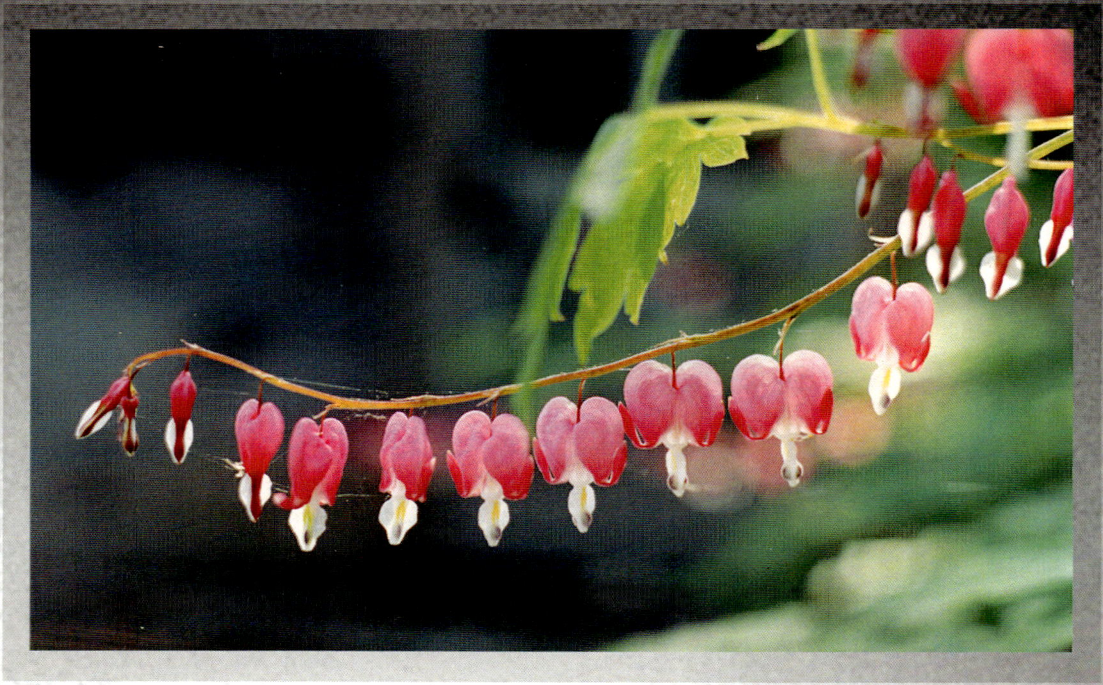

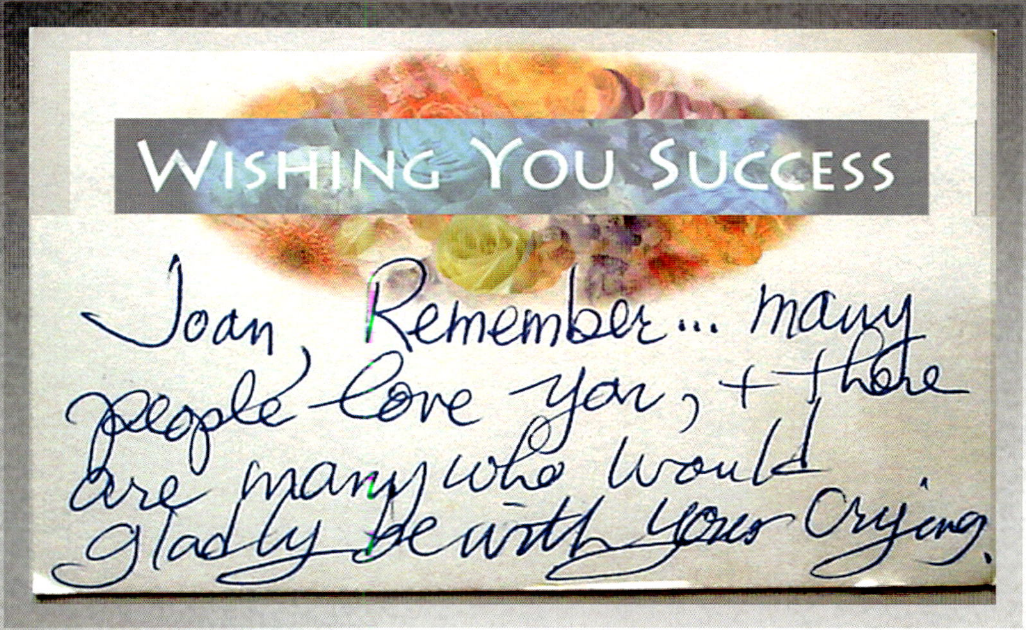

Joan, Remember . . . many people love you,
& there are many who would gladly be with your crying.
(*back*) GOOD love is worth the wait, & you'll know it.
MOM IN ME

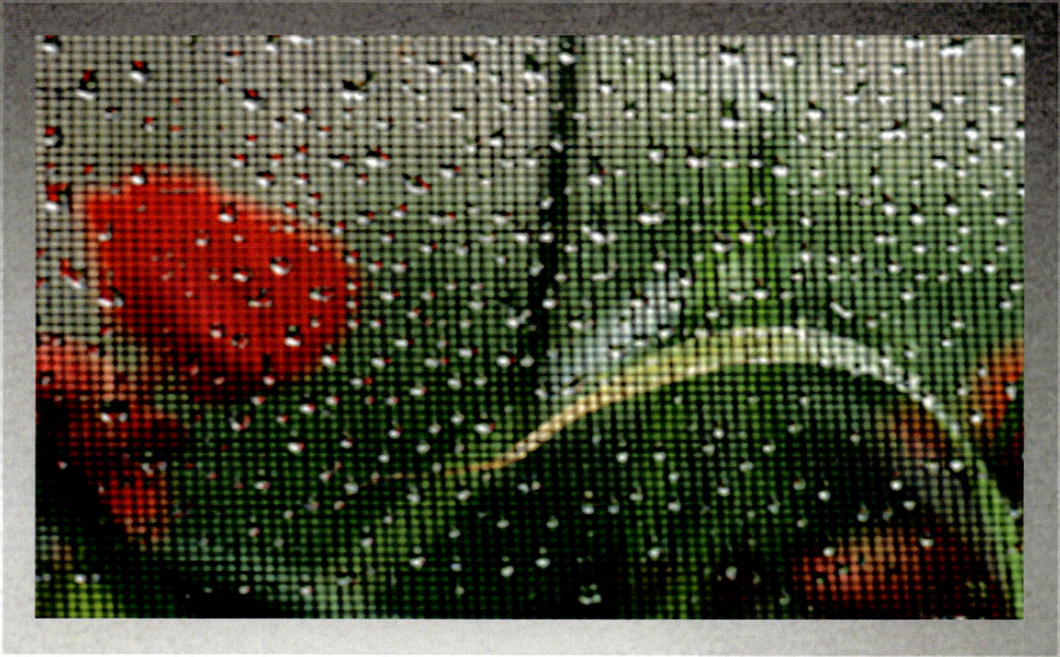

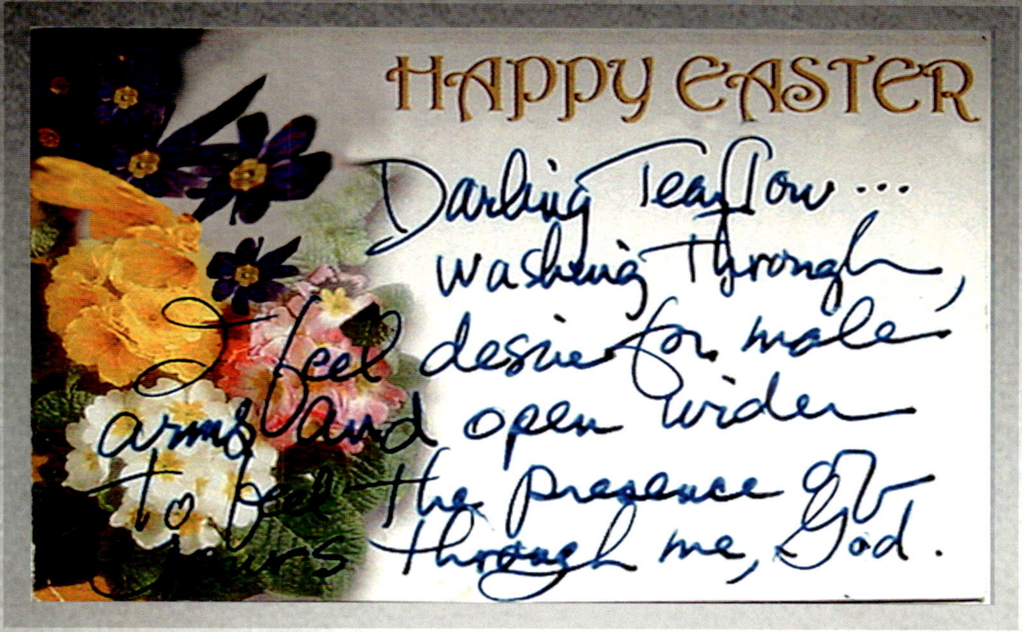

Darling Tearflow . . . washing through,
I feel desire for male arms and open wider
to feel the presence of yours through me, God.

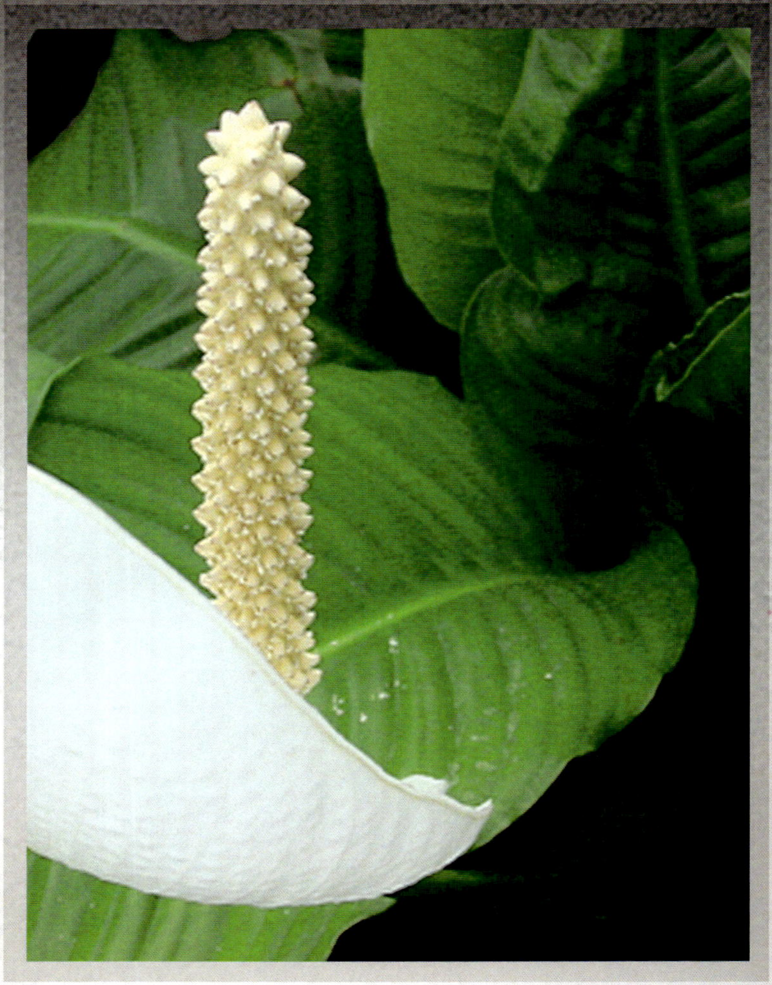

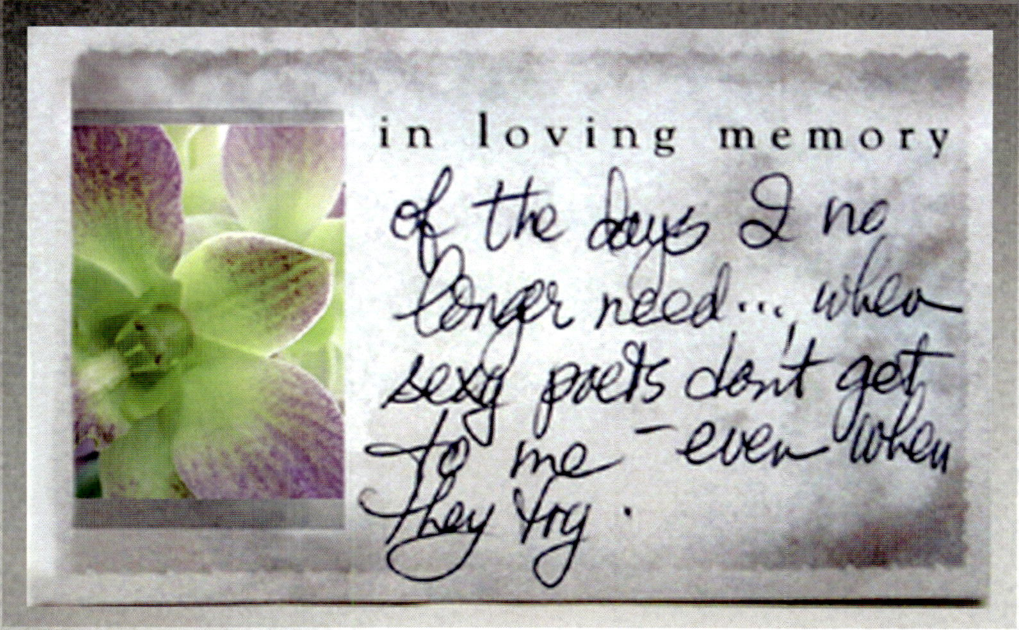

In loving memory of the days
I no longer need . . . when
sexy poets don't get to me —
even when they try.

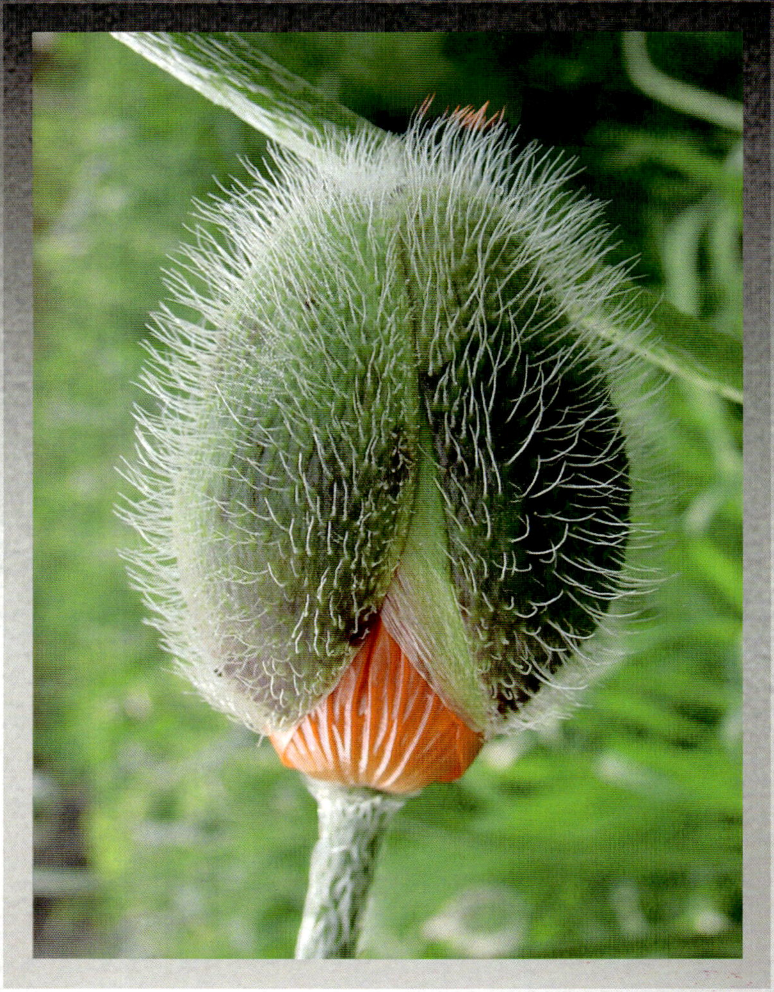

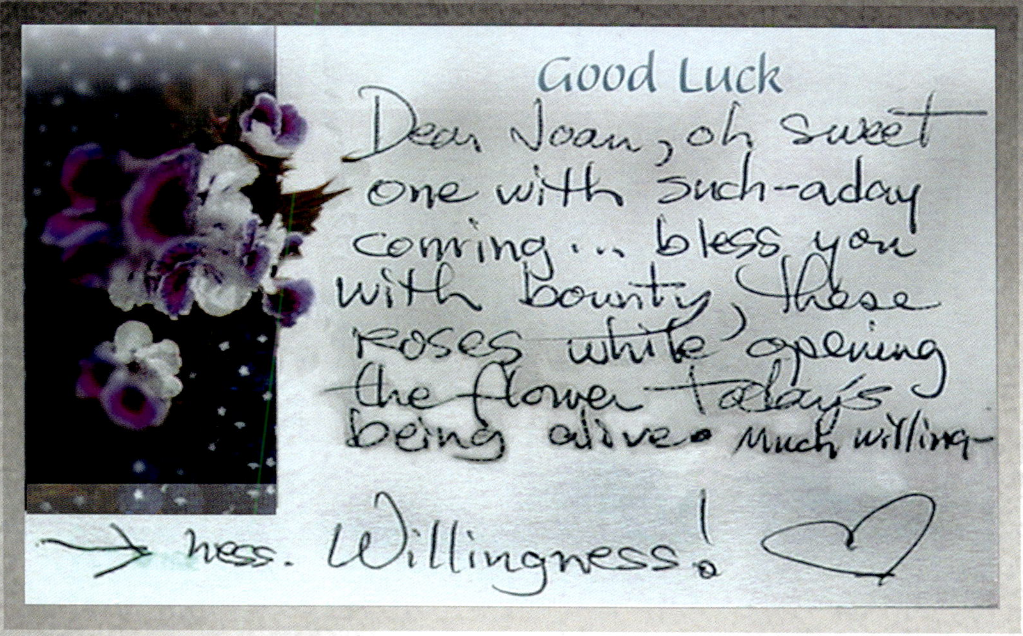

Dear Joan, oh sweet one with such-a-day coming . . .
bless you with bounty, these roses while opening
the flower ~ today's being alive. Much willing -
→ ness. Willingness !

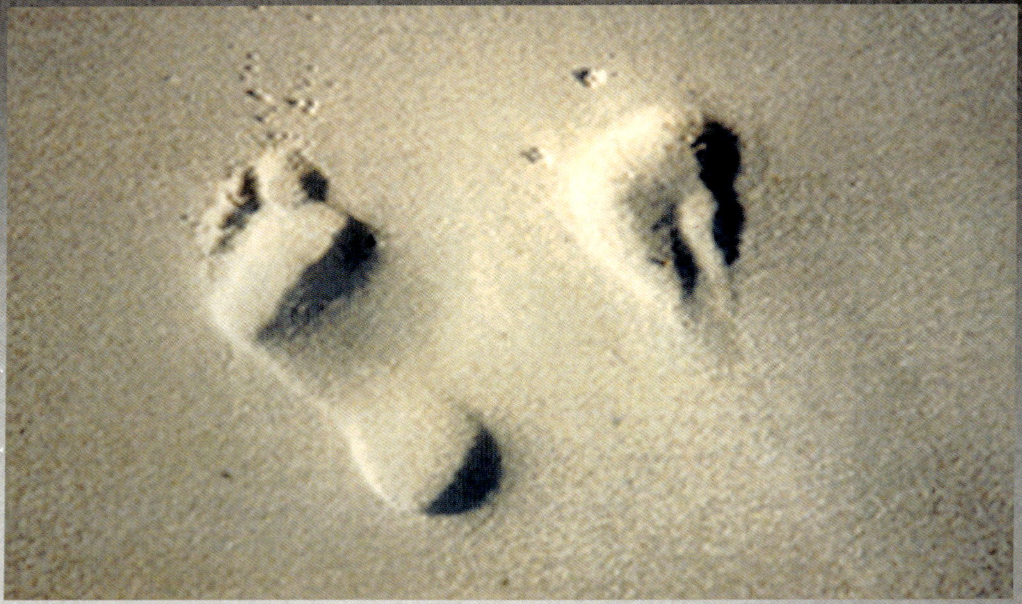

photo by Alan Burr Steinbach

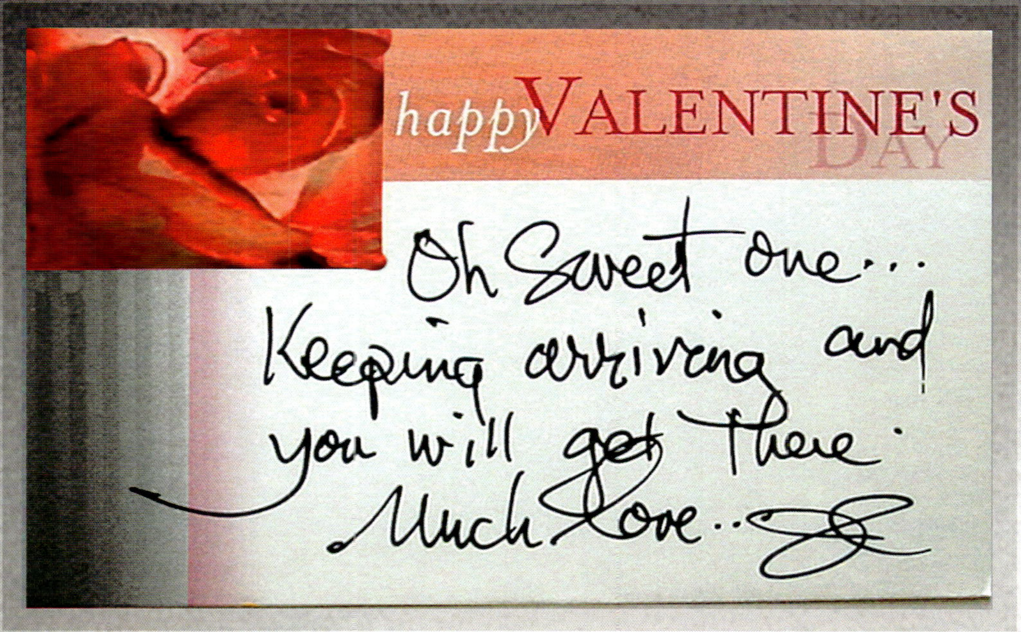

Happy Valentine's Day
Oh Sweet one . . .
Keep arriving and you will get there.
Much love . . . JL

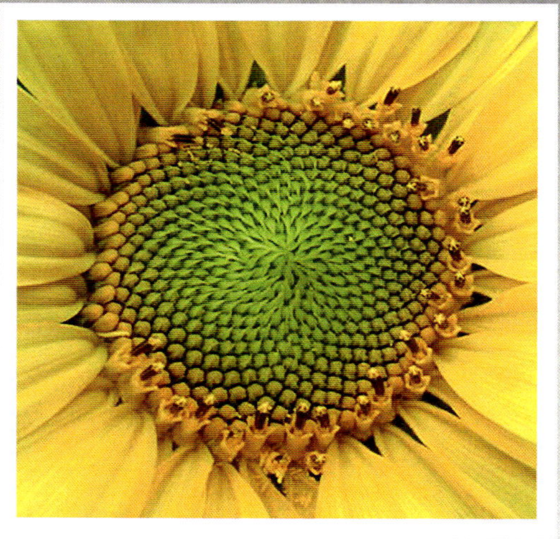

Flow

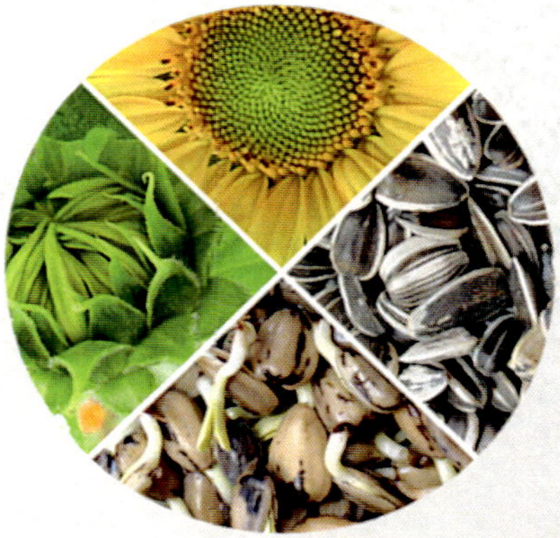

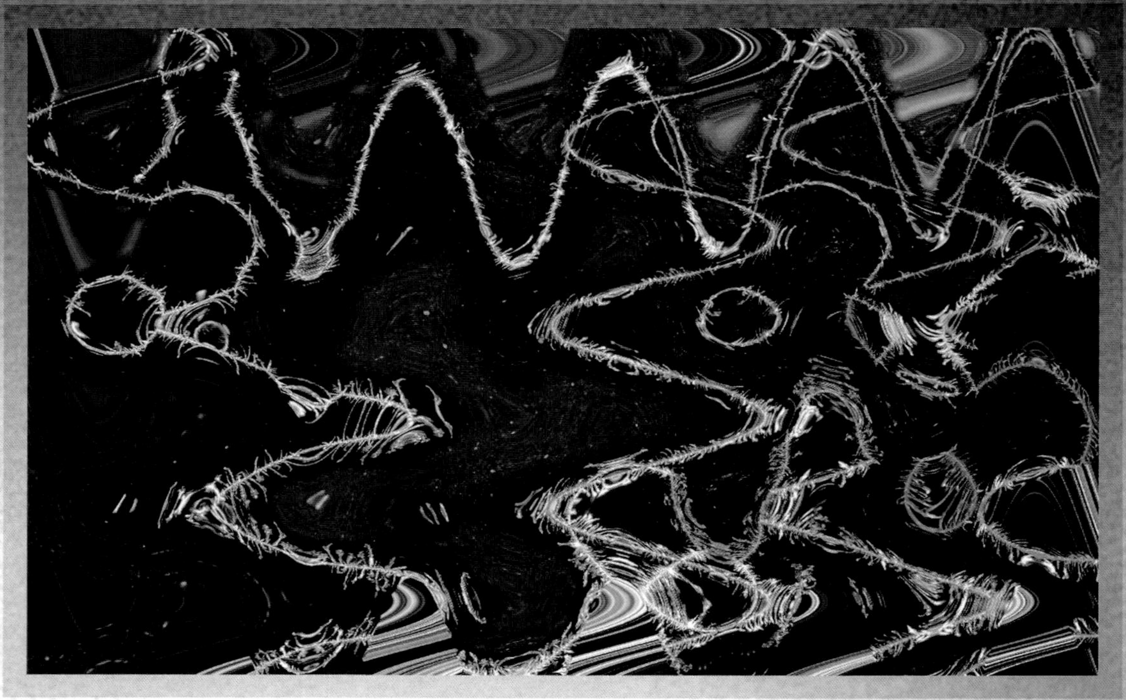

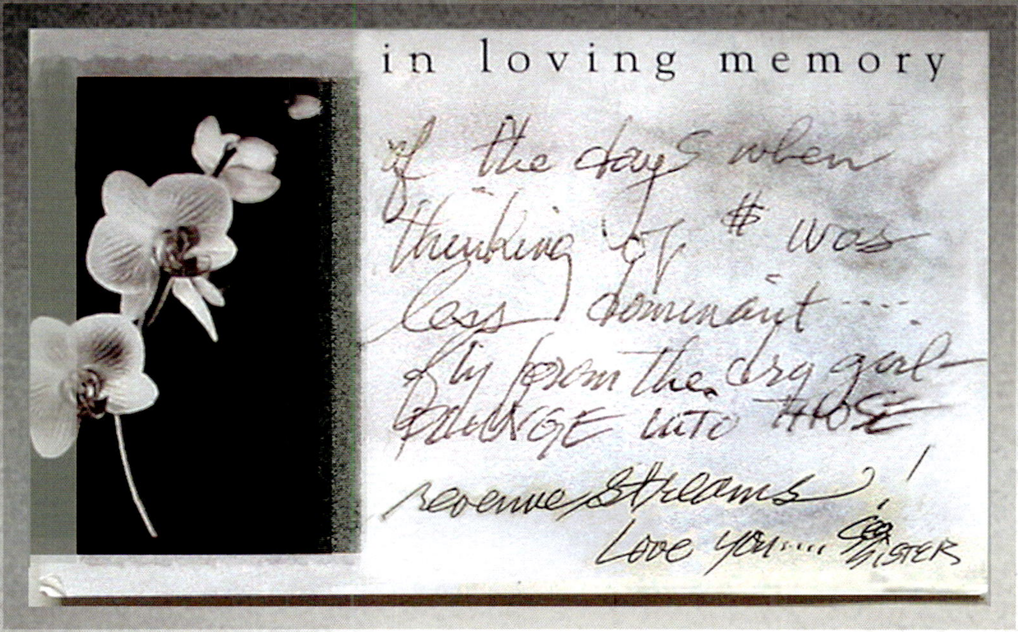

In loving memory of the days when
thinking of money was less dominant . . .
fly from the dry girl –
PLUNGE into those revenue streams !
Love you . . . Sea SISTER

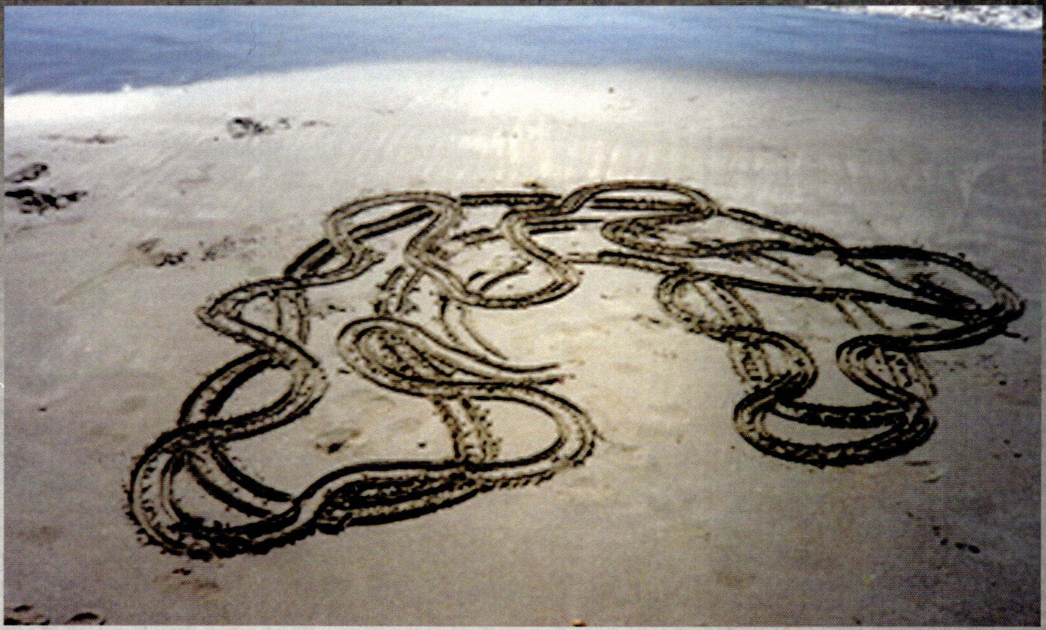

Photo by Alan Burr Steinbach

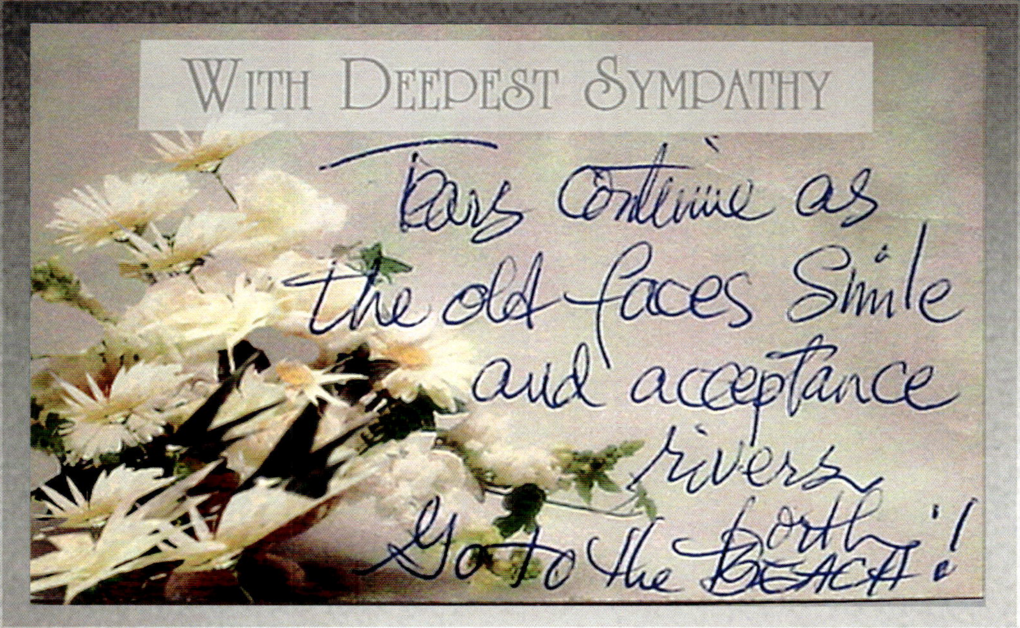

Tears continue as the old faces smile
and acceptance rivers forth.
Go to the BEACH !

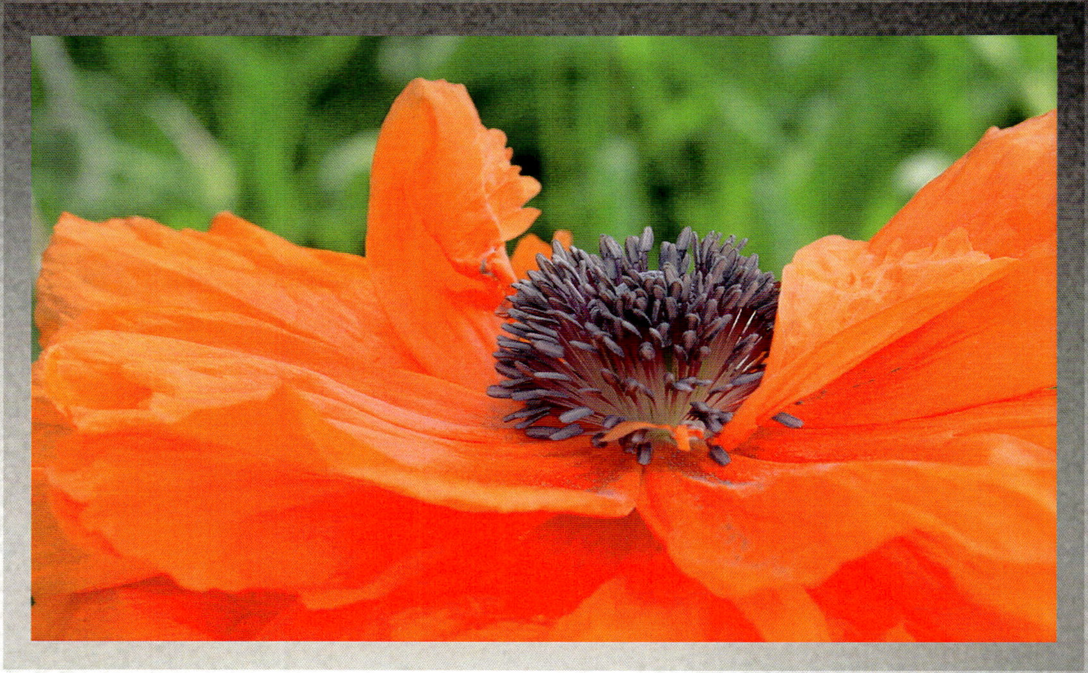

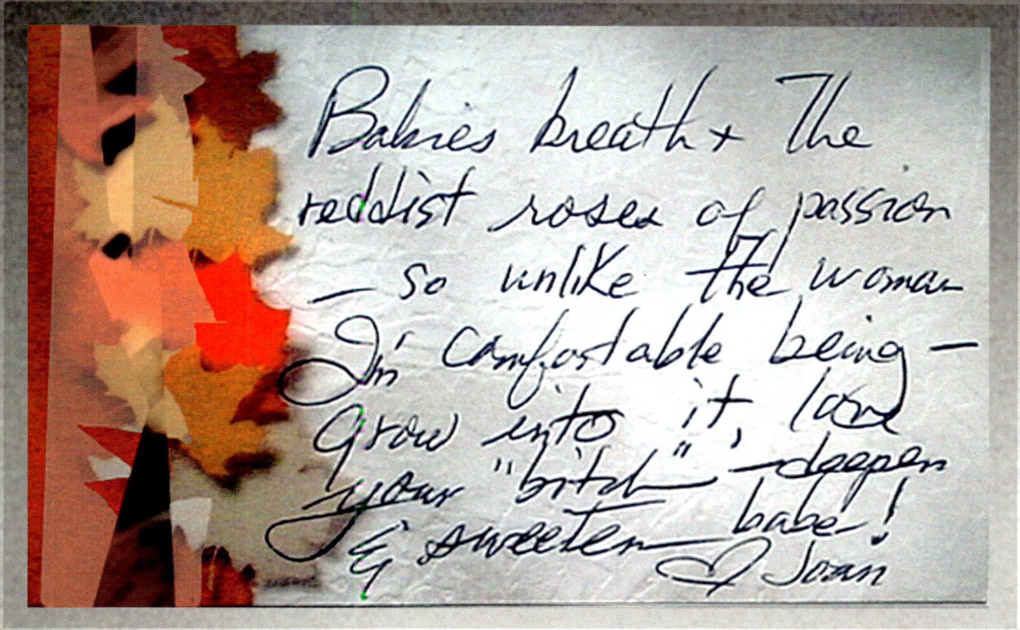

Babies breath & the reddist roses of passion
— so unlike the woman I'm comfortable being —
grow into it, love your "bitch"
deepen & sweeten babe !

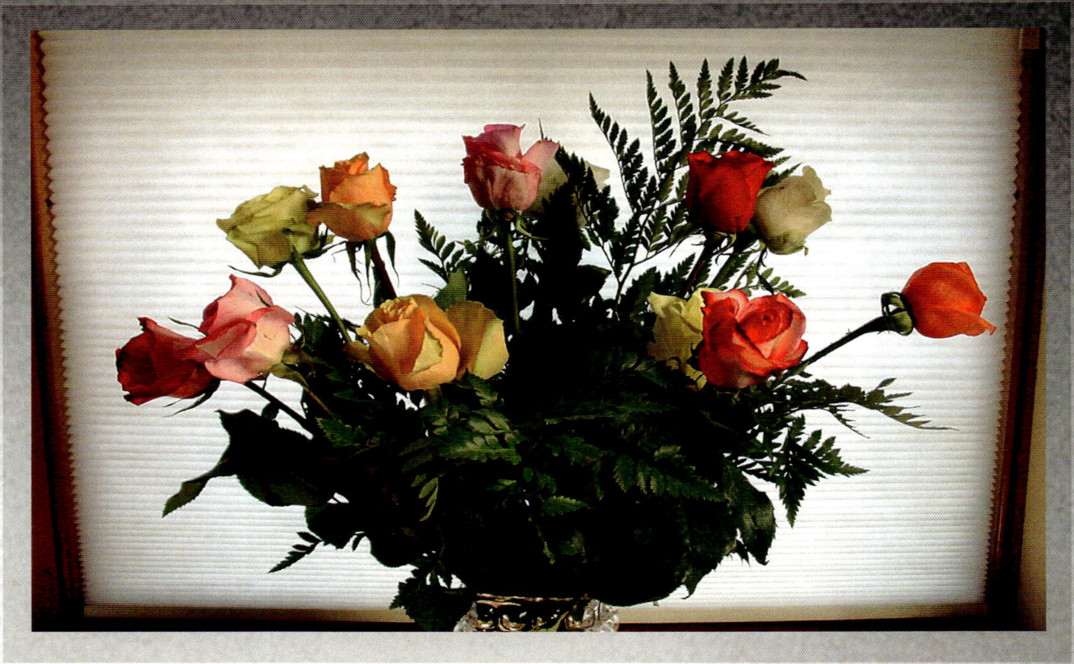

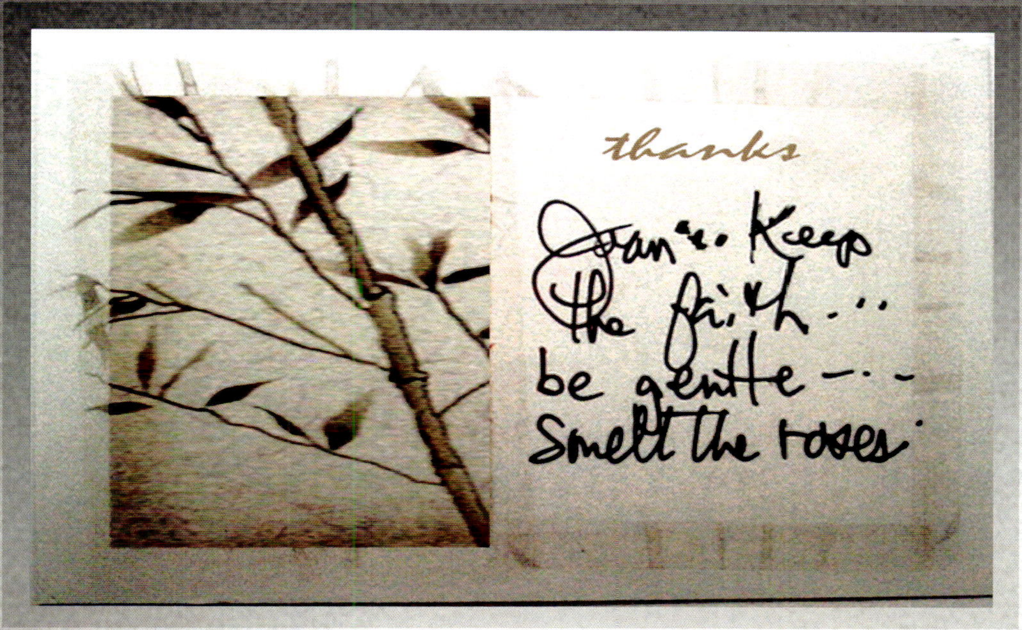

Joan . . . keep the faith . . .
be gentle ~ · ~
smell the roses.

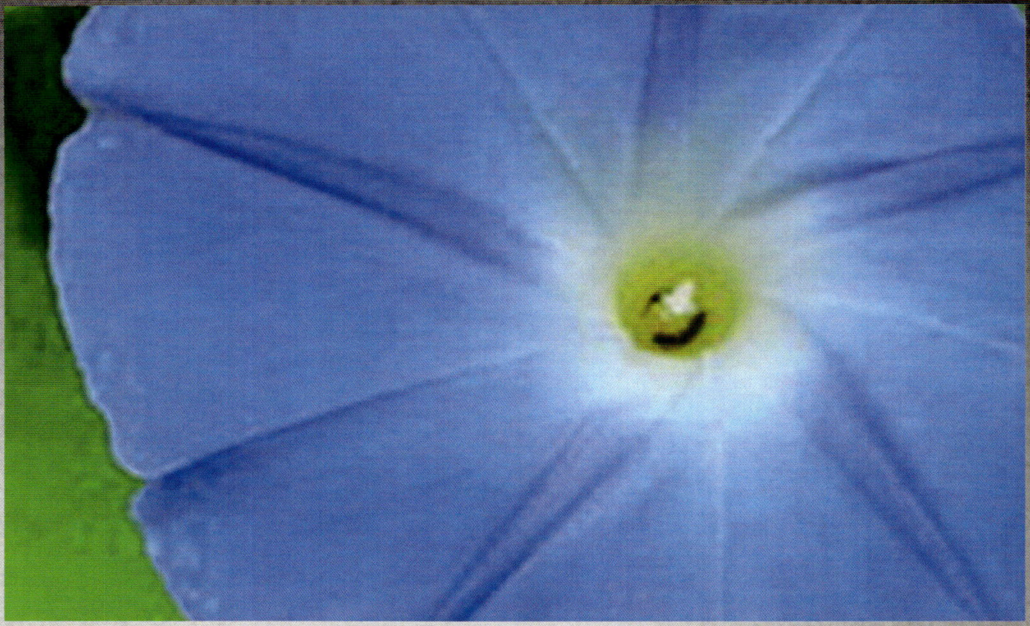

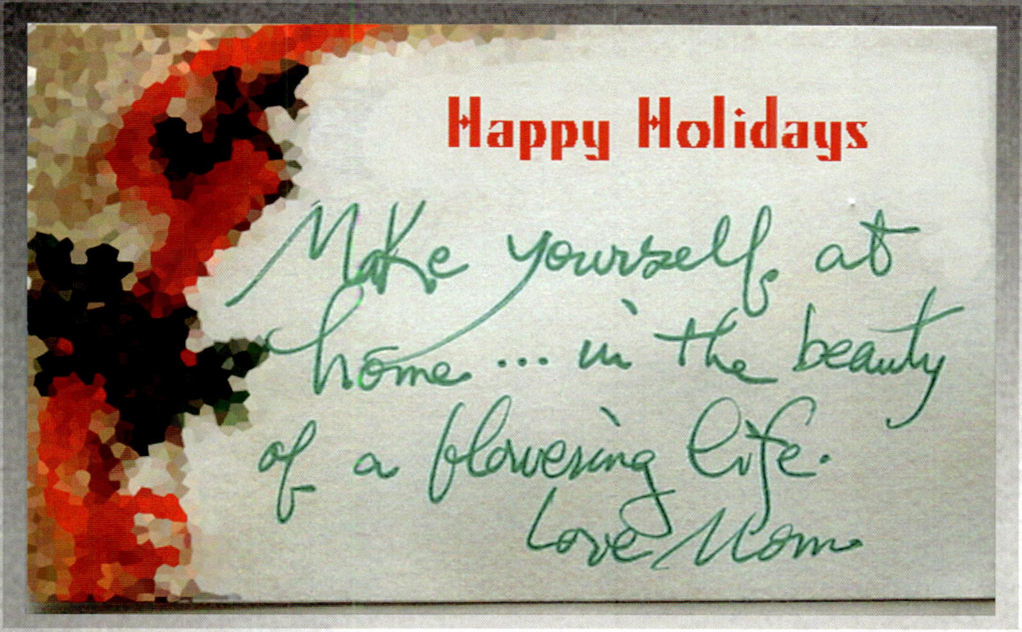

Make yourself at home . . .
in the beauty of a flowering life.
Love, Mom

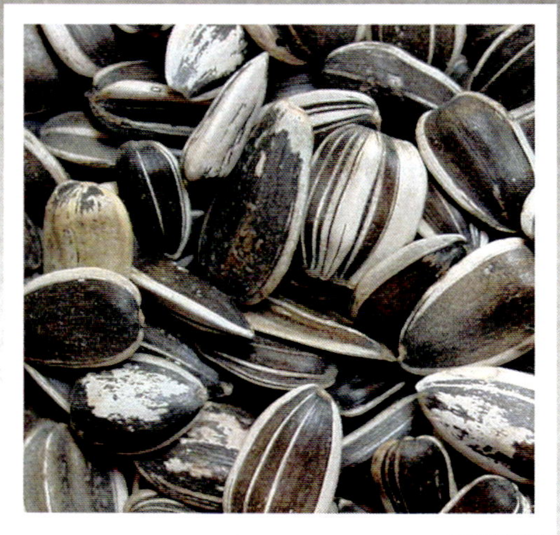

Cycles

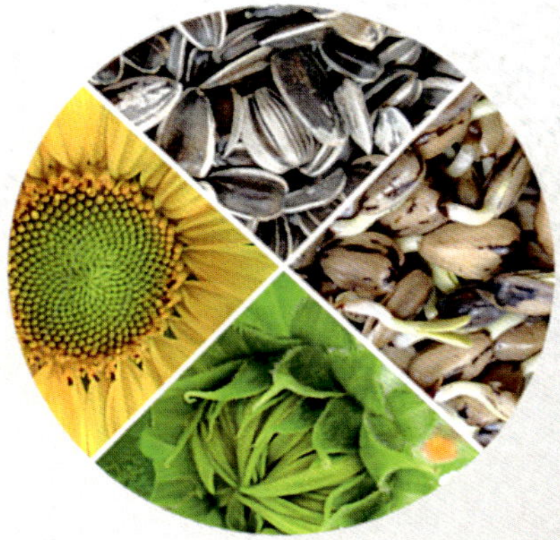

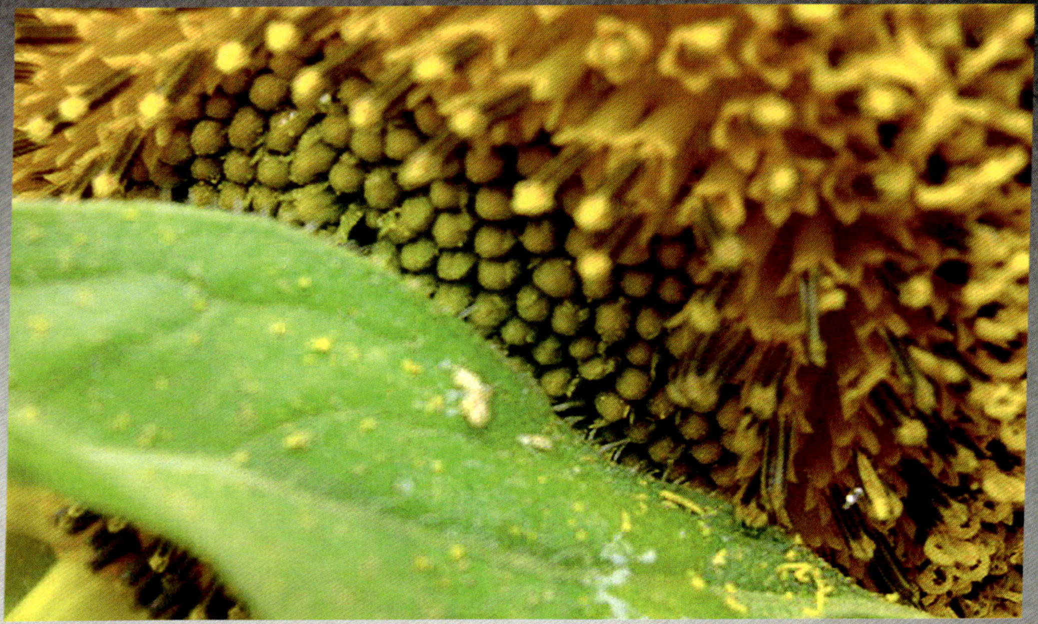

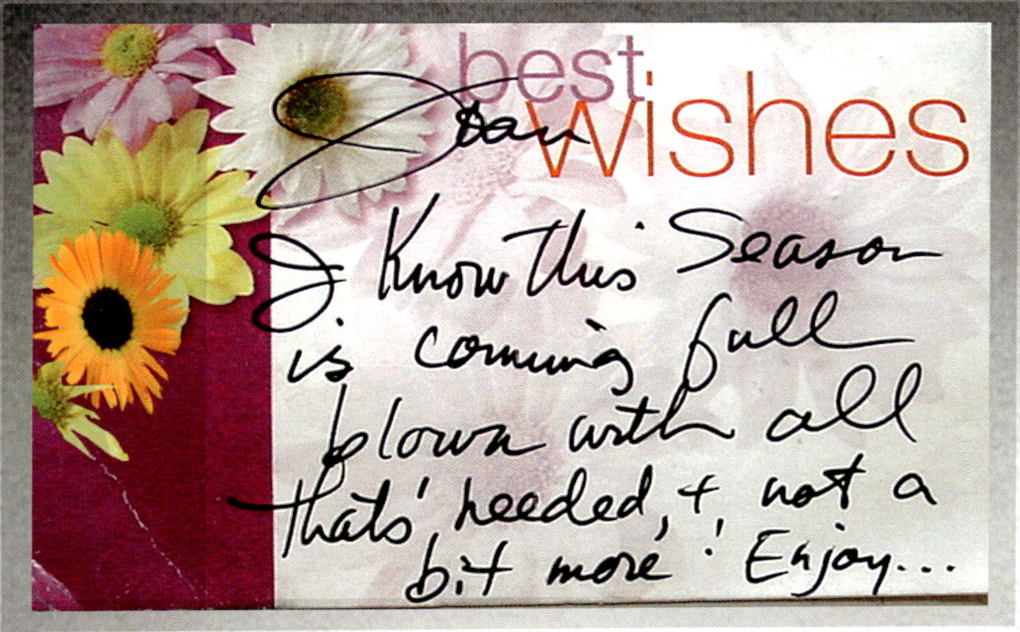

Best wishes Joan,
I know this season is coming full
blown with all that's needed,
& not a bit more ! Enjoy . . .

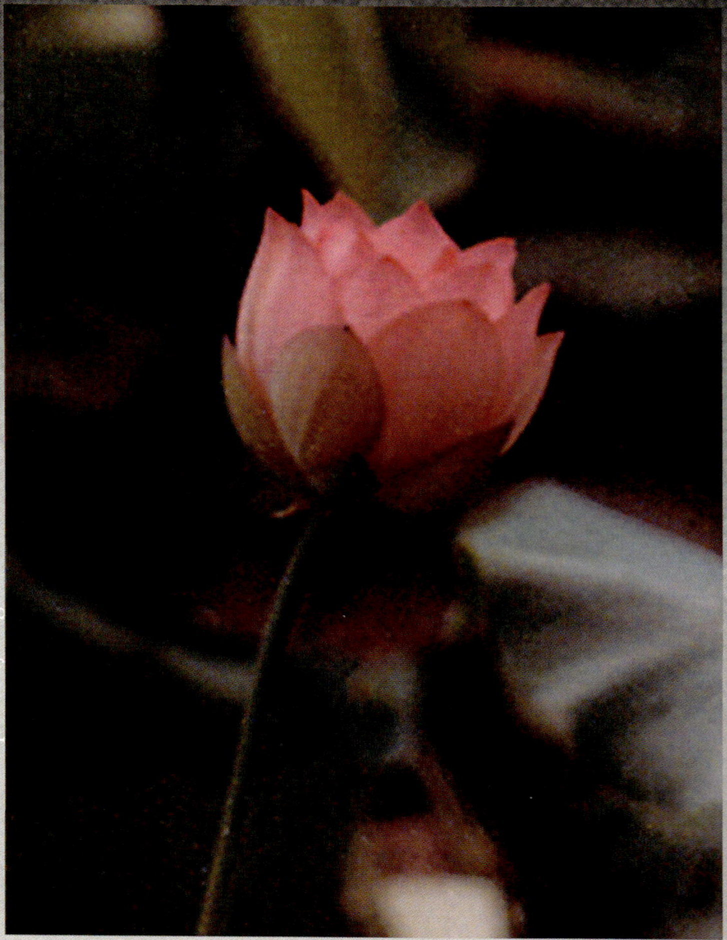
detail of photo by Roger Ide

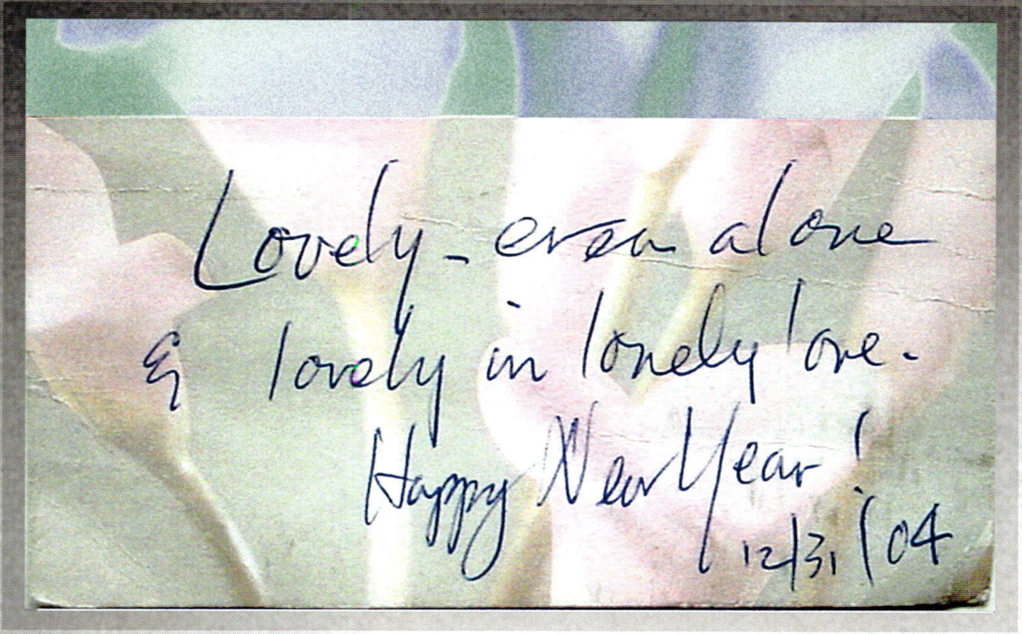

Lovely – even alone
& lovely in lonely love.
Happy New Year !

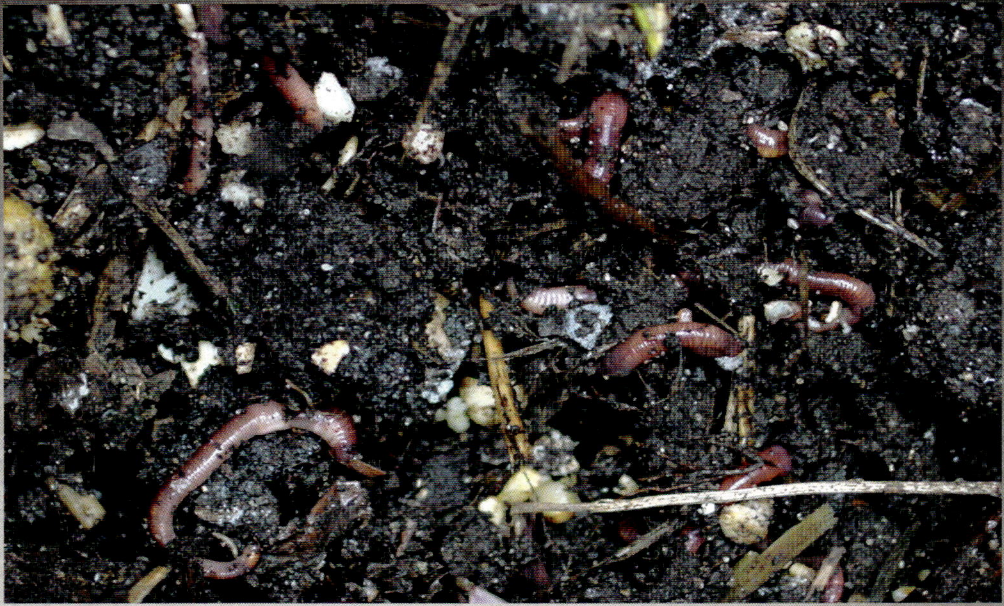

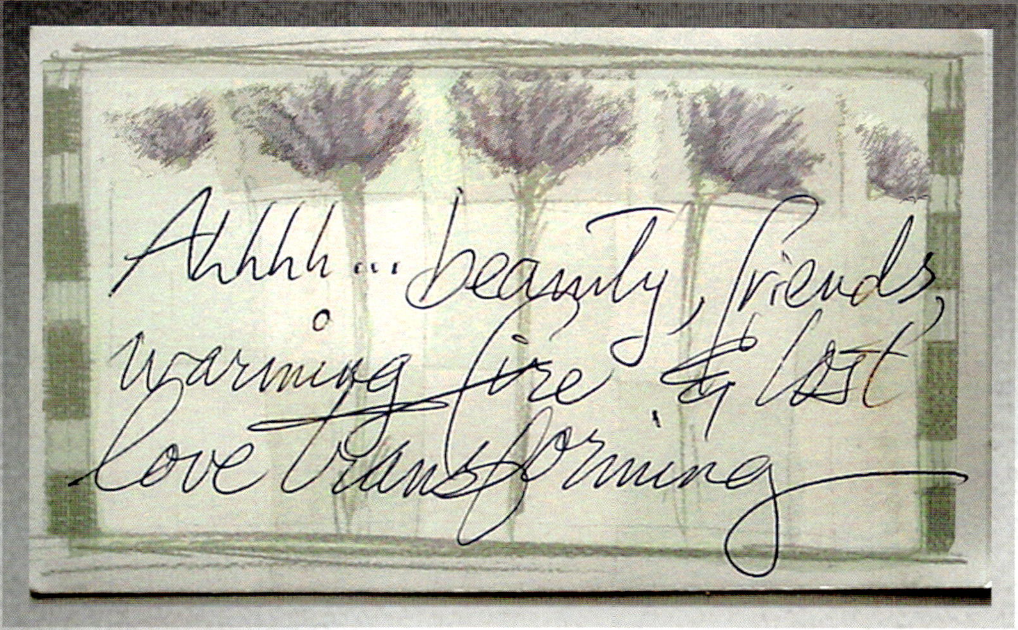

Ahhhh . . . beauty, friends,
warming fire &
lost love transforming.

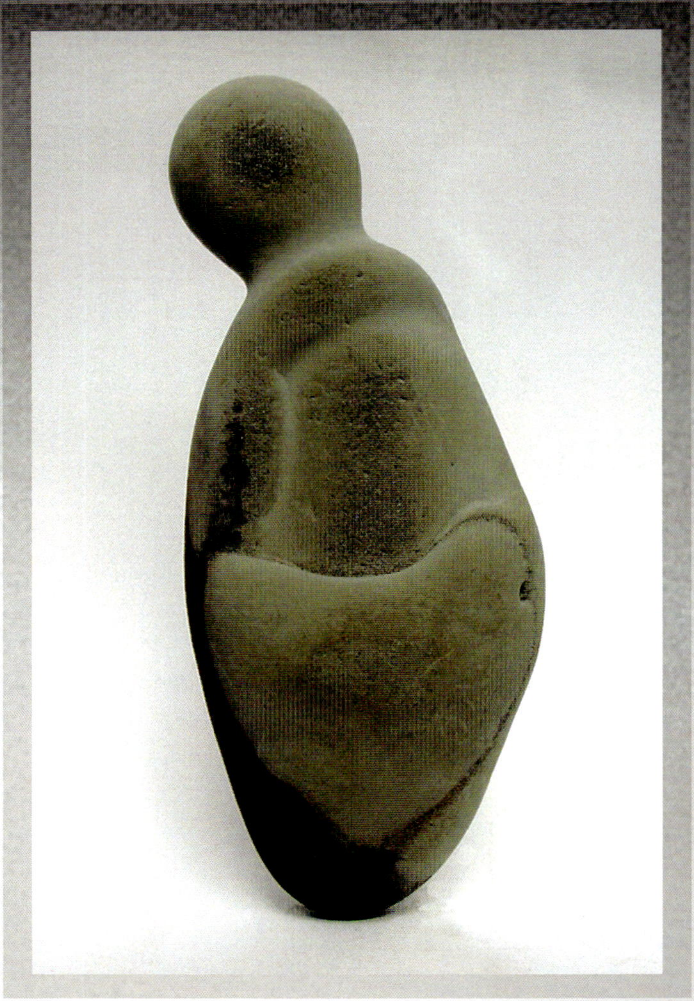

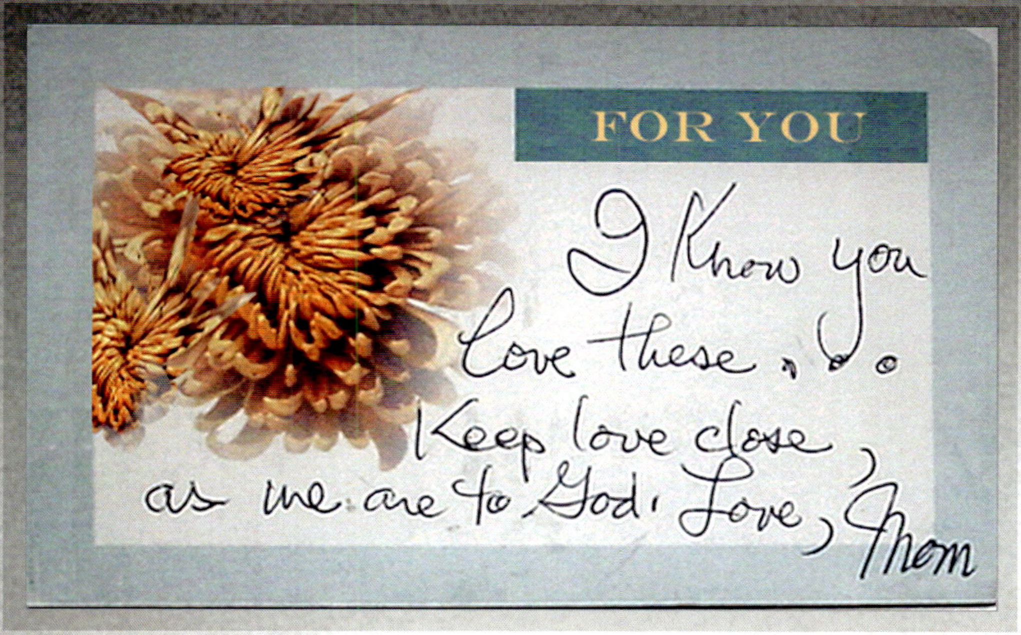

I know you love these . . .
Keep love close,
as we are to God.
Love, Mom

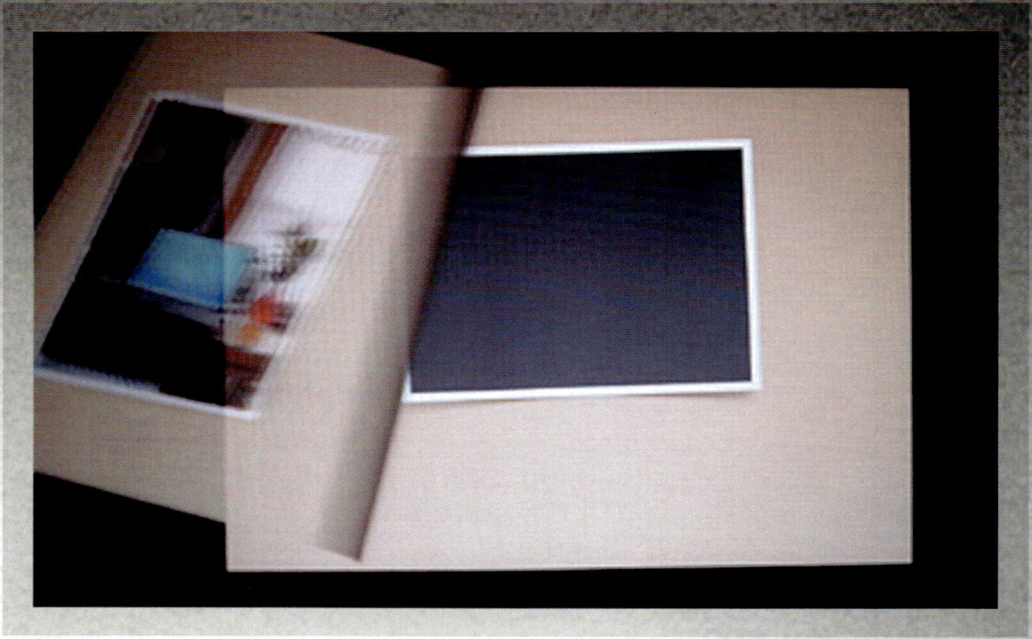

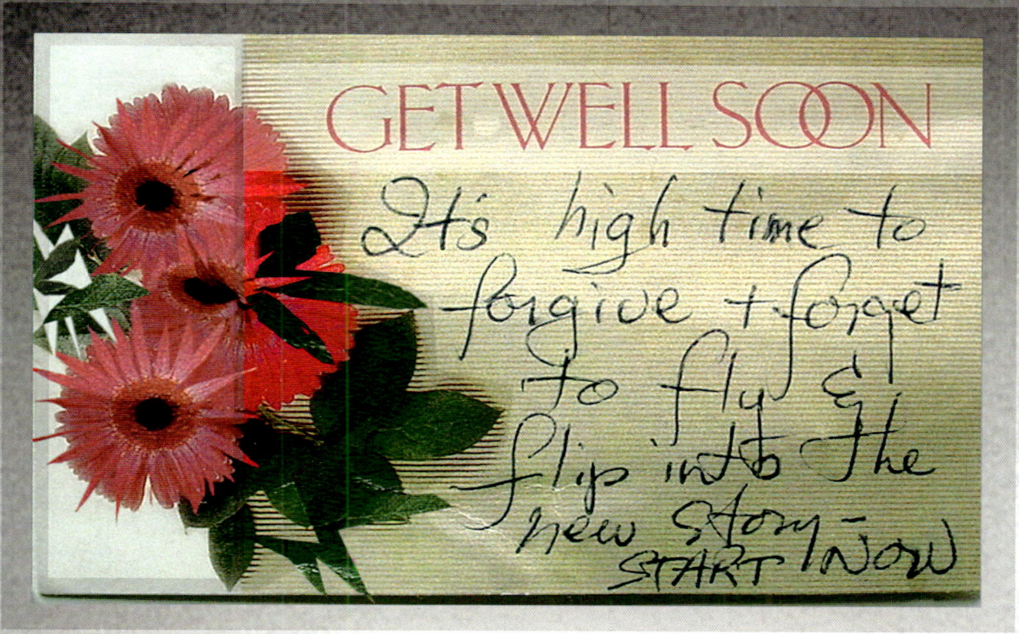

It’s high time to forgive and forget
– to fly & flip into the new story –
START NOW.

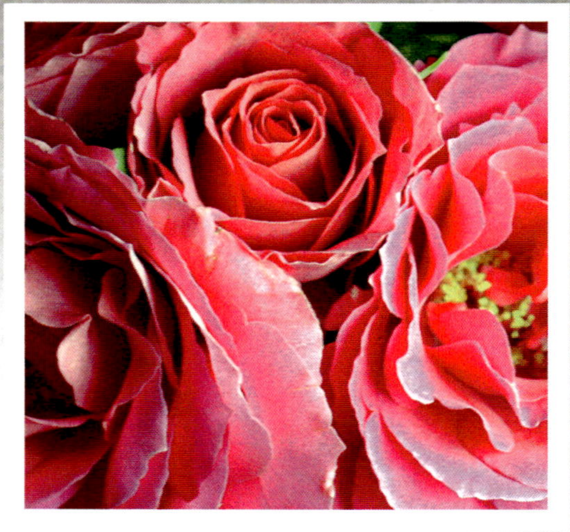

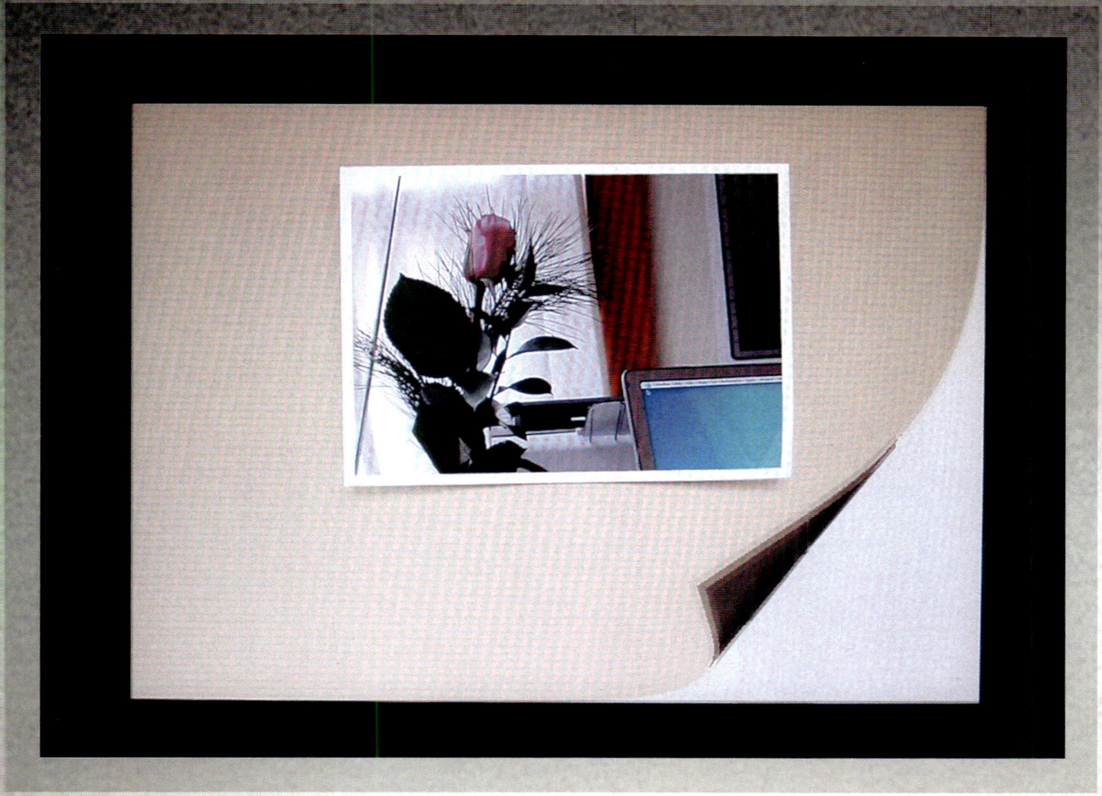

Notes

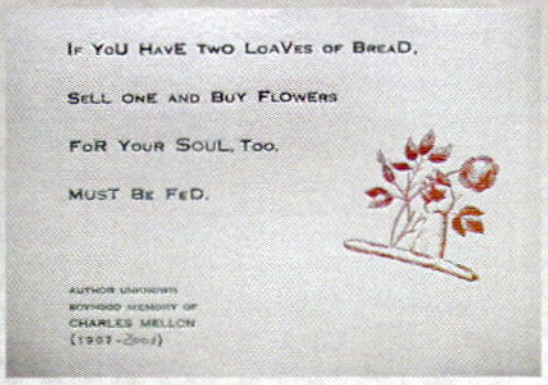

14 Arleen Mellon made this card using the quote, a boyhood memory of her father Charles Mellon. Author unknown. Side image is a hand holding roses, rising from a baguette. It's a letterpress print from Bluestocking Press, St. Helena California. Arleen sent it to me before she knew I was making this book.

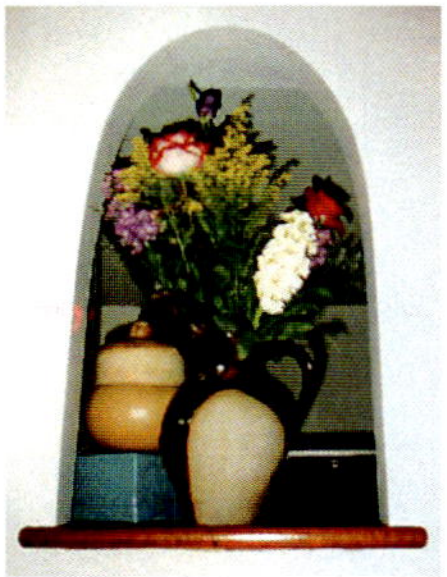

18 This still life formed after Perry Lederman's memorial service on Father's Day 1995, at the entrance to our home. A gourd jar held crying cloths. The blue box held his cremains. A "butt pitcher" came to the ceremony filled with flowers from Candy Proctor. These memories were framed by the opening in a wall I made years before, according to catenary arch principles of kiln design.

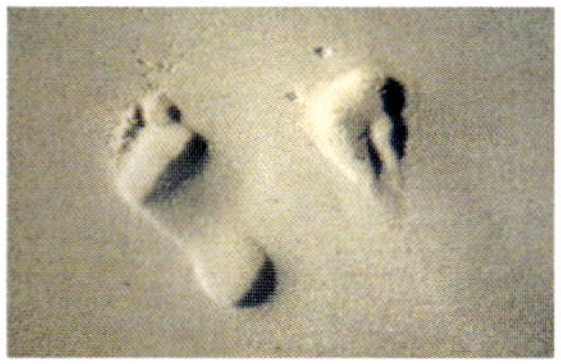

34 & 40 Alan Burr Steinbach kept a camera protected and available for such moments of everyday pleasure like the light on his footprints and on his sand drawings with two sticks, or was it a forked one?

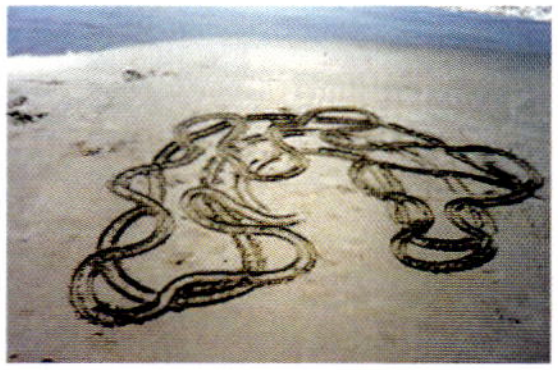

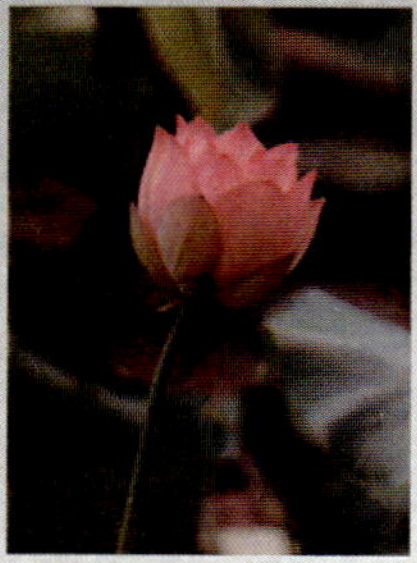

52 The pond on Juniper Point in Woods Hole filled with lotus for a very few years, and Roger Ide took photos for me. This one flower is a cropped image from Roger's bigger landscape.

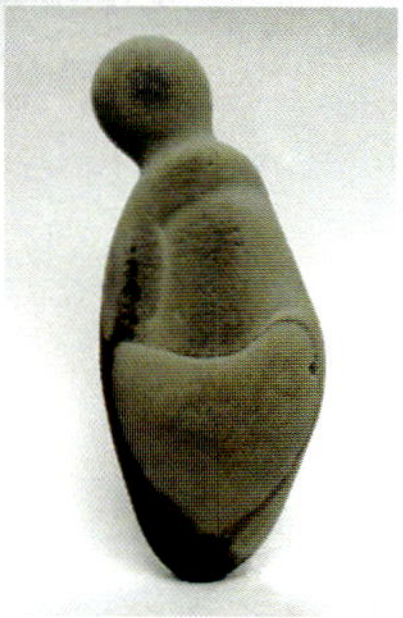

56 This concretion is a sedimentary material that formed within the muddy bottom layers of the Connecticut River. It was mined by Holland Hoagland who slipped her arm into and under layers of silt. She gave me this one because of the mother and child image. No human hands shaped it.

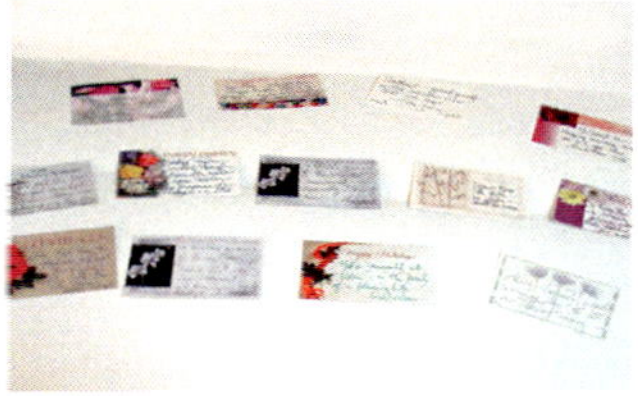

Thanks to Capri and their designers of cards available at the market. In the letter of copyright law, I believe I changed them adequately. In the spirit of giving due credit, I wanted to both use the cards and alter them, which I did using the powerhouse software, Photoshop.

All Other Photos

Photos not mentioned in these notes I took, including sunflowers grown in my seaside garden, compost brewed from kitchen gleanings, and frost crystallized on my windows.

Acknowledgments

Making a book seemed possible after Betty Jean Wall and Rolland Fischer showed me how they made books. In addition to practical help, they nourish me with inspiration, humor, and love.

Generous editing and proofreading were given by Julie Lipkin, Molly Bang, Mary Swope and Betty Wall. Samm Carlton's broad-brush choreographer's view of the whole helped me counter balance focus on details. Special mention of how Astrid Erodahl's way with flowers makes shopping for groceries a heartwarming experience. Keeping things in perspective by laughing was easier after I heard Elijah Wald say, "Perfect is the opposite of done."

Unknowingly and importantly, several animals helped by bringing together Roberta Ornstein and Rayna Lederman at a dog park in Boston. Their friendship led me to Eric Rosenberg, who helps me concentrate by overseeing some financial issues.

Many people I haven't named have helped and will help, just by being who they are. It's so simple.

Special thanks to Earth, whose lessons inform my livlihood as a potter, and to the people who buy my work . . . which gives me the gift of time to continue creating.

Postscript

Some unintended consequences of making this book:

I've been reminded of my food preferences of more than two decades ago, when I grew and ate many kinds of sprouts. Eating condensed potential always attracted me and now I'm reviving that custom, and returning home to my own plant nature by sprouting leafy greens, beans, grains, nuts, and seeds.

Surprise surprise, on the day I finally assembled files for printing, I reached the end of the computer's hard disk space. Final files were duplicated on an external drive, but I when I tried to burn a disk of the biggest asset folder from which I built pages of this book . . . *poof!* Five and a half gigabytes vanished and were transformed into an alias on the desktop, with no sign of original files anywhere. How apropos with my decision to shred the flower cards and envelopes used in the book . . . this last image.

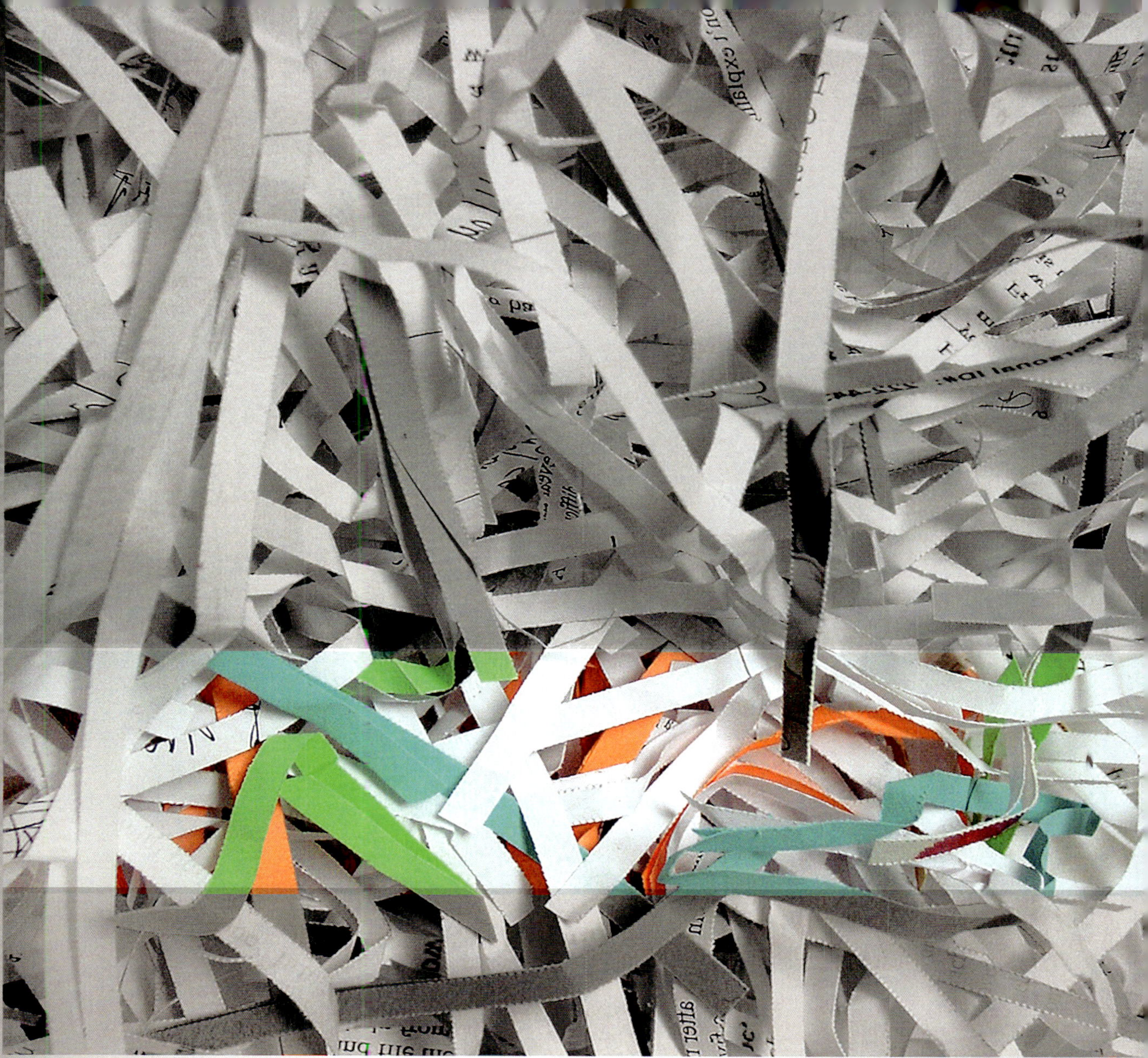